A Guide to Growing Your Business

ARMINLEAR

A Guide to Growing Your Business

Proven Methods for Entrepreneurs, Marketers and Sales People with No Time to Waste

William D. Hughes
with Aastha Verma and Michael Hughes

ARMINLEAR

Cover Design by C.S. Fritz

ARMINLEAR

Armin Lear Press

825 Wildlife

Estes Park, CO 80517

ISBN 978-1-7354650-9-8

Introduction

From the moment we wake up, we're surrounded and inundated with marketing promises and claims. A big reason for the relentless messaging is that we "carry" myriad vendors with us in our smartphones. They push information at us, and we pull in what we want—hour after hour.

If your business has serious sales goals and you're in a hurry, you need to drive faster than the competing traffic. With no time to waste, this book narrows its focus on what matters, makes sense and makes money. This translates into targeting the right customers with products that solve important problems and makes people feel smart and good about becoming your customer.

With that, you can transform your business plans and vision into the rapid-response business you promised your customers, investors, family, and yourself. Chapters focus sharply on the need-to-know instead of the nice-to-know.

If you are an entrepreneur in a start-up, statistics suggest your chances of succeeding aren't great. This book will help you avoid the new-business cemetery. You do that with tight market focus, product differentiation, and by building relationships with your target customers.

As ex-heavyweight champion turned mass-market BBQ grill salesman George Foreman says, "Learn how to sell. You'll never starve."

The chapter on behavioral economics explains why so many customer decisions are puzzling and irrational. That doesn't stop people from making them, of course, so understanding customer motivation gives you a distinct advantage in the marketplace.

In addition, the Internet has become the most powerful marketing weapon in history and the COVID-19 pandemic made it a mandatory component of our business life. Technology has changed how we live, how we communicate, sell, buy, research, learn, and play.

Google unveils sellers' costs and secrets. Armed with high-powered computers (aka smart phones), today's customers know more about what they are buying than they did back in the twentieth century. Alibaba presents your products to prospects all over the world and describes them in the buyer's native language. And it's only just beginning as Cloud Computing, Artificial Intelligence, Machine Learning, Big Data, Block Chain, and more become more commonplace.

The technology section will help you become tech savvy and give you the firepower to leverage technology and make most everything work better and happen faster. Both of my co-authors have extraordinary technical business credentials and know better than most anyone how to use the Internet to gain a competitive advantage. Michael is a nationally known search engine and Internet marketing expert. He's been in the on-line marketing business for twenty years and worked with thousands of businesses and web owners. Aastha is the ultimate technical program manager and is currently managing one of our nation's most critical cyber-security and critical infrastructure projects.

In all, this book is for business professionals with lots at stake and no time to waste. Time to start making changes and start making money!

GETTING STARTED

Chapter 1: Getting Started

One way to get started is to quit talking and start doing.

- Walt Disney
Walt Disney Company Founder

Start by doing what's necessary; then do what's possible, and suddenly you are doing the impossible.

- St. Francis of Assisi
Patron Saint of Italy in 1228

Marketing makes change. Sales make money.

Many people think of marketing as advertising. Others think of marketing as a fancy word for selling. Still others view it as having something to do with market research. Then there is the street-smart view that really does capture what marketing is and does, namely: You stand a good chance of succeeding if you figure out what people want in the first place.

Marketing

Marketing is the matchmaker between what your business is selling and what customers desire and buy. To that end, marketing makes change happen.

Marketing begins with an idea about a product or customer need. Marketers conduct research to uncover actual needs, trends, and opportunities. They analyze the competition, determine price and packaging, establish distribution channels, and create/execute promotions to stimulate demand.

Actually, marketing is more encompassing than that. It's everything you do that involves the public. It's how your people answer the phone, the way you present your invoices, your returns policy, and how you treat everyone who encounters your business. Marketing is not a part time or emergency measure: It must be planned, budgeted, and measured.

Done right, marketing creates awareness, uncovers the best prospects, and stimulates them to want what you sell; that is, marketing creates demand for your product or service. Sales picks up where marketing leaves off. It starts with marketing and moves into selling.

Sales

When selling to other businesses (B2B), relationships are your priority. Here, the story behind the product is often more important than the product. When selling to consumers (B2C), it's about traffic.

Selling begins when people become aware of you and your product. They become prospects if they are interested enough to allow you to try and convince them you can solve their problem. Next, they start thinking seriously about your product; then they begin to imagine themselves owning it and start to want it. Ultimately, they buy.

Making a sale is not the end. A sale is just the beginning—the beginning of what can be a long and prosperous relationship for both parties.

Activities that shorten the sales cycle, that cause orders to occur faster, have the biggest payoffs. But aren't most sales and marketing activities supposed to make sales happen faster? The answer is "Yes," but some address the challenge much more directly than others.

That's why direct response advertising is more effective than indirect, awareness advertising. It's why demonstrations and samples work better than brochures. (Those people giving away bits of sausage at Costco whenever we don't have a virus pandemic are worth their weight in dollar bills for the manufacturer.) It's why asking for the order in person always works better than asking over the phone.

When something is important enough, you do it even if the odds are not in your favor.

- Elon Musk
CEO Tesla and SpaceX

Mistakes

When companies struggle to meet their business goals, here are six of the most common and costly reasons why.

Common Business Mistakes	
Unprofitable Business Model	Expenses leave no room for profit.
Wrong Target Market	Going after markets where the market leaders are entrenched.
Poor Positioning	Products need to be different, not better.
Lousy Sales Force	Fix this and you can live with some of the other sins.
Inept Digital Marketing	Search engine and social media marketing are not optional.
Distribution Channels	See below.

Distribution Channels

Recently someone asked me to name the most critical part of a sales and marketing plan, that is, what matters most? Advertising? Quality products? Good service? Prompt delivery? Plenty of cash?

All of them matter, of course, but I would not identify any of them as mandatory. I was tempted to answer, "A great product," but I thought about all the successful companies whose products are just ordinary.

Providing a path for prospective customers to do business with you may be the most important thing you can do. If you do not have a convenient way for customers to buy what you sell, everything else is futile. This can be a store, a sales force, a distributor, the Internet, mail, television, radio, or drone. Somehow, you must give customers access to your products.

Good salespeople in the right places, a quality network of dealers or distributors, an online e-commerce presence—they all work. With the right sales infrastructure you can overcome just about any obstacle to generating revenue. Invest in your sales organization, both the people and the infrastructure that allows them to reach customers.

And never stop recruiting. You always need good salespeople. Hire the right ones—those with strong interpersonal skills, a healthy sense of risk, and a grasp of what motivates your target customers—and you can turn a mediocre business into a real winner.

Some people talk about a dream but don't follow through. Others make it happen.
What's the difference? HUNGER. Hunger gives you drive—not talent, not skill.
With enough hunger you'll find a way.

- Tony Robbins
Author, Motivational Speaker

Wrap Up

Pick a target market that is small enough for you to afford to make a splash and where the competition is not entrenched.

Hire superstar sales professionals; you'll sleep better at night.

Chapter 2: Assessment: Where are you?

Change before you have to.

- Jack Welch
Former Chairman and CEO of General Electric

How would you describe your current business situation? Where are the gaps? The opportunities? Where will change pay off? If your business isn't growing, it's dying.

Note to start-ups: Considering the uncertainty of a start-up business, you can waste valuable energy and time in refining a detailed business or sales plan. You need a plan, but you do not need to get into the weeds of detailed planning. You are better off relying on proven tools such as a Strengths, Weaknesses, Opportunities, Threats (SWOT) analysis and then following it with an action plan outline. Try the Fast-Pass Worksheet near the end of this book as the SWOT follow up. The reason for proceeding this way is that entrepreneurs' initial ideas and actions almost always need tweaking and changing. Expect to make changes on the fly and be prepared to do that.

Failing to Plan equals Planning to Fail

First the big picture. Start with a SWOT analysis, an organized list of your business's greatest strengths, weaknesses, opportunities, and threats. Recognize that whatever got you to where you are today is probably no longer sufficient to keep you there.

Strengths and weaknesses are internal to the company (think: reputation, patents, location). You can change them over time but not without some work. Opportunities and threats are external (think: suppliers, competitors, prices)—they are out there in the market, happening whether you like it or not. You can't change them.

Existing businesses can use a SWOT analysis, at any time, to assess a changing environment and respond proactively. New businesses should use a SWOT analysis as a part of their planning process. Your chart will look like the one below:

	Helpful	Harmful
Internal Present	Strengths	Weaknesses
External Future	Opportunities	Threats

Situation Today

Next, take a closer look at your situation today.

	Declining	Steady	Growing	Don't Know
Sales				
Profits				
Receivables				
Customer Count				
Your Market				
Your Industry				
Your Competition				
Your Business				

Business Model

Before we go any further, let's make sure this business can make money. You'll need what's known as a Proforma Income Statement (P&L), which is analogous to a monthly budget. It looks like this:

Monthly P&L – Based on cash collections and payments		
Revenue	What you've collected from sales of your products or services to customers during the month.	Let's assume $10,000
Cost of Goods Sold (COG)	This is what the product cost you to buy or make or what you had to pay the people who delivered the service	Say $4,500
Gross Profit	Revenue minus COG. This is what's left after you pay for what you sold.	Leaves $5,500. This is the most important number. Too low and you can't afford the below.
Overhead	Rent, Utilities, Insurance, Operating Expenses.	Fixed cost. Keep as low as possible. Let's say $2,500
Salaries	Pay you and your associates	15% or $1,500
Pre-Tax Profit	The bottom Line	15% or $1,500

Pay attention to the Gross Profit. It is the number that drives the business. And watch the overhead. Keep it at the planned rate.

Wrap Up

Create your business model and SWOT analysis. Get going. What needs to get done now?

Chapter 3: Goals

"There ain't a horse that can't be rode.
And there ain't a cowboy that can't be throwed."

- Texas Ranch Wisdom

Goals should be quantitative so that progress is measurable. Measurements should be under your control and verifiable. Instead of having a goal of 10 percent market share (something you really can't count), translate that into selling a specific number of units at a certain price in a defined period of time.

Goal setting is always a valuable exercise, even if you don't have enough time to validate every assumption. At least you'll be thinking about the right subjects—like sales, margins, expenses, and profit.

Action

Doing what you've been doing is going to get you what you've been getting. Where are your best chances for growth and improved business results? Don't worry about the future—shape it. Plan on what you know, can predict and what customers will crave. Make it simple and doable. Start with just a few action items that can be executed in a month or two.

High expectations are the key to everything.

- Sam Walton
Walmart Founder

Business Culture (Soul)

Successful businesses have an intangible energy that inspires enthusiasm and mutual purpose. Researchers have determined there are three major factors affecting this. Winning businesses have:

- *A loftier reason for existing other than revenue growth and profits.*
- *Powerful and ongoing customer connections.*
- *Employee autonomy and creativity.*

Mission Statement

Mission statements are grand proclamations and not typically found in sales and marketing plans. However, at their best, they do capture the corporate soul.

I've never found a universally accepted definition of what a mission statement should be or even its purpose. Some think it should paint a picture of the future. Others think a mission statement is how you differentiate your business from the rest. Others think of it as a slogan.

I've even heard smart businesspeople claim that a mission statement shouldn't be made public because doing so tells competitors where you are going. Customers, they say, don't care about the future; they care about what's in it for them now.

To confuse the issue further, people, who are supposed to know about these things, talk not only about mission statements, but also about value propositions, vision statements, and—as a marketer my favorite—positioning statements.

I think a mission statement should justify the business or organization's existence. Its purpose is to distinguish the business from others. It should be specific, easily recalled, and provide direction. Finally, it should be followed by objectives to fulfill the promises, and strategies and plans to make it all happen. For example,

- *Google's mission is "to organize the world's information and make it universally accessible and useful."*
- *Shopify's mission is to "make commerce better for everyone, so businesses can focus on what they do best: building and selling their products."*
- *Uber's mission is to bring transportation – for everyone, everywhere.*
- *Our mission statement for this book is "to help our readers make money faster than they would have if they hadn't read it."*

The greatest danger for most of us is not that our aim is too high, and we miss it, but that it is too low, and we hit it

\- Michelangelo
Italian Renaissance sculptor, painter

Sales and Marketing Check List

- **Sales**

  Recruiting your own Salespeople or Resellers

  Training – Product knowledge, Sales strategies and tactics, Pricing, Terms

  CRM, Forecasting

  Territory, Target Markets, Target Accounts

  Quota

- **Marketing**

  Target Market Clarity

Differentiation

Messaging

Lead Generation

Digital

Wrap Up

Make a Who, What, & When List of Goals for the next few months **W**ho's responsible, for **W**hat, and **W**hen will it happen). Make each goal measurable, doable, meaningful, and deliverable in the next month or two.

PRODUCTS

Chapter 4: Products

Instead of finding customers for your products,
find products for your customers.

- Seth Godin
Author, *This Is Marketing*

Selling products, services, or knowledge all require different sales approaches. Products are tangible, services less so, and knowledge is elusive.

- **Products.** You are selling something that's been manufactured, and the customer will take possession of and own like equipment or specialty furniture. In the digital age, a lot of products have physically nothing in common with an office chair, but they can be defined in terms of features such as performance, benefits, quality, and durability—the same features used to evaluate an office chair. When you concentrate on those features, you can stay in close touch with customer expectations.
- **Services.** Now you are selling something you perform for the customer, for example, cleaning services or equipment installation. Focus on uniqueness and credibility. Customer expectations need to be controlled, so be as clear as possible on what you will deliver and make sure it is documented. Unlike product sales, these customers

can walk away if they are not satisfied. So, stay close to the customer, which may mean finding occasions involving interaction. Don't take the timesaving, easy way out and have a Zoom meeting when you can sit in the person's office and have coffee together.

If it's a fixed price contract, beware of "scope creep" (when the customer realizes midway through that he/she forgot something). If the project is very large, changes are inevitable so both seller and buyer should plan on that. This means the customer should be prepared to spend something beyond the initial amount, but you need to become adept at cost containment; try to keep the additional amount to no more than10 to 15 percent. Make sure the customer understands that adding new services adds more cost.

- **Knowledge.** Here you are selling innovation and know-how. You provide the customer with information such as an organizational plan. This is more of a team effort—the customer brings the problem and its unique characteristics; the seller brings experience and know-how.

To simplify the conversation, in this book, think of what you're selling as a product even if you're selling services or knowledge. Let's look at the factors you must consider in successfully moving your product into the marketplace.

Differentiation

Many of your prospects will have to go to their bosses and explain why they chose you. Unless you're a clear, dominant market leader with revenues and profits to prove it, do not claim "yours is better than theirs." That's because, with that point of view, you're putting your product in the same category as all the others, so the win potentially goes to the market leader.

Instead, focus on what makes you different and what matters most to the client and/or what aspect of the client's needs you meet particularly well. You want your prospect to represent you as a company that specializes in solving their kind of problems. With that in mind, you need clear answers to:

- What problem does your product solve? Clarity about what marketplace problems you're solving positions you to succeed in your sales and marketing efforts.
- Who has that problem? Identifying who needs products like yours give you the language to craft customized benefits statements for prospects.

People buy feelings, not things. What you make is fundamentally important, but whether anyone will buy it depends on how the product—and you—make them feel. And especially now in a landscape crowded with options and messages, customers tend to have very short attention spans. Don't make them have to think about what your product will do for them. Your answer should be short and memorable—about twenty-five words should be enough. Give your customers something to think about other than price.

Differentiating yourself in the marketplace means spotlighting what you do best. That action is mandatory when you're just one of many selling against much larger and better-known competitors. Use the differentiation to shorten your sales prospect list and minimize lost business.

I was running sales in the western US for a high-tech company. I had sales offices in most of the bigger cities. All performed reasonably well except the one in Denver, Colorado. I even considered closing it when one day I got a phone call from one of our competitor's best salesmen in Los Angeles. He told me he was moving to Denver and wanted me to hire him to sell our products there. "Why Denver?" I asked. "What do you know about the area?" He told me he had never even been there. I dug deeper. His girlfriend was moving there, and he told me he couldn't live without her. I hired him.

Normally, I would have sent a new salesperson back to our East Coast headquarters for product training. In this case, my new salesman, who was very experienced selling products like ours, told me that would be a waste of his time and our money. All he needed from me was to tell him what our product did best and, therefore, what customer problems our product was best at solving.

He proceeded to Denver without the training, and for the first two weeks, never left the office. Instead he did research and identified the top one-hundred companies in that metro area that might need what we sold. He then got on the phone, called all of them, got to a person or department that bought what we sold and asked each if they had problems like the ones, we were best at solving. Eighty said no. Twenty said yes.

Over the next three months he visited all twenty. By the sixth month, he made more sales than all the sales we had made in Denver during the prior three years. Tight market focus pays off and as I said, hire great salespeople—people who are hungry to succeed—and *you* will be a superstar.

Presenting Deliverables

What do you deliver to your customers? What do they get when they open the door or open the box? Describe your product or service in concise terms. Avoid adjectives. "The monitor you ordered is enclosed" conveys the message that the customer is receiving what the customer asked for. "A slate black, state-of-the-art, adjustable monitor is enclosed" says nothing of value and may even make the customer wonder, "Was that what I ordered?"

What else does your customer receive beyond the basic product, for example, an instruction manual, warranty card, telephone support? Include intangibles such as prestige. Your cover note with the delivery could say, "The monitor you ordered is enclosed along with a warranty card and contact information for customer service and technical support."

If your deliverable is a report, the same kind of cautions apply. A report prefaced by a lengthy introduction about the meticulous methodology that went into it leads the customer to think, even subconsciously, that you are offering excuses for some shortcoming in the report by focusing on how you created it.

Pricing

What is the product's retail/list price, average discount, the cost of making/delivering the product (cost of goods), and the resulting gross margin? When your product is sold direct to an end user, that's one thing. When it's going through a distribution channel (reseller) that adds a layer of complexity and a probable reduction in margin. Price the product for the end user, leaving enough margin for you to offer the reseller a healthy discount.

Intellectual Property - A Competitive Advantage like Few Others

We marketers are always looking for a competitive edge. Unfortunately, most competitive advantages tend to be short lived, that is, competitors quickly counter with matching functionality, something better, or easier to use, and/or cheaper.

On the other hand, intellectual property (IP) is one business asset that cannot be duplicated by your competitors. Intellectual property can be a brand, invention, design, a song or any other another expression you have created.

IP needs to be considered from day one of your business. Do a search for your proposed new business name and brands. You'll need to use names not being used by someone else. By doing so, you're not just protecting your own brands, you're also making sure you're not infringing on others' brands.

IP comes in many flavors. Patents protect inventions. Design registrations protect the ornamental features of a product. Trademarks protect business names and brands. Copyrights protect the expression of an idea, which potentially includes website content, brochures, technical manuals, and written promotional material and images. Trade secrets are just that, *secret* exclusive information such as customer lists that provide a competitive advantage in the marketplace.

Patent: This is a time-limited monopoly granted to an inventor by the federal government (twenty years for utility patents and fourteen years for design patents). To receive a patent, an invention must be "novel," "non-obvious" and "useful."

Trademark: This is the name—very often the brand—used to identify and differentiate a product. If a trademark is regularly used and does not become a generic term, it can be renewed and kept in force indefinitely.

Copyright: This protects written documents such as books and plays, as well as music, films, and other creative works from being copied. A copyright is valid for the life of the author plus 70 years.

Service Mark: As the name implies, it pertains to a service. Among the best-known service marks are American Express's Don't leave home without it.® and KFC's We do chicken right.® Like a trademark, a service mark can be renewed on a regular basis and kept valid indefinitely.

Trade Secret: Some companies have formulas or processes that are exclusively theirs, and rather than patent them, and having the patents run out, they keep them as trade secrets.

Having your own trademark is a good intellectual property first step. Create your own prospective trademark and then search the USPTO's trademark database (Trademark Electronic Search System, or TESS) to see if any trademark has already been registered or applied for that is 1) similar to your trademark, 2) used on related products or for related services, and 3) live. A trademark that meets all three criteria will prevent your trademark from being registered because it creates a likelihood of confusion.

In addition to providing you with a marketing edge, IP can also dramatically affect your net worth and corporate valuation. Investors and venture capitalists are most attracted to firms with IP. In fact, often they are more interested in the company's IP than they are with the actual product and/or income statement.

If your business has proprietary aspects and products, you obviously need to protect them from being replicated by your competitors. Regardless of all the precautions you may have taken, such as copyright and trademark notices or confidential markings, you never know who is going to read your plan. If you are going to share your business plan with others, be careful. If your product includes proprietary intellectual property, do not disclose it in the plan. Only disclose such data, under controlled conditions, to the right audience at the right time. When you do disclose it, even if it is informal, use a Non-Disclosure Agreement (NDA) to protect yourself. An NDA, also often referred to as a confidentiality agreement, is a legal contract that restricts access to your proprietary information to the party signing the NDA. For a free NDA, go to www.rocketlawyer.com.

Wrap Up

- What makes your product different?
- Protect your IP legally.

Chapter 5: Customers

Companies, markets, and offices don't buy anything. People buy.

You need a composite picture of your typical customer to sell anything. Don't treat this lightly and give it a quick brush because you think you know all about your customers. You can't know too much about the people who will make or break your business.

A friend of mine who ran a small professional theater did an analysis of the people who were subscribers. She found that most of them had been subscribers for years and had a strong sense of loyalty to the company of players, type of plays, and even to the unique theater space where productions were mounted. One of the couples who were subscribers became embroiled in an acrimonious divorce. Rather than have tickets to her theater become a source of anxiety, she ordered the box office to issue each member of the couple an additional subscription ticket and assign the couples to different nights. Word of what she had done got around in the community and the number of season ticket holders rose immediately. The perception was that the theater was as loyal to its customers as the customers were to the theater—with "loyalty" being a core concept in customer appeal.

Since no two customers are alike, consider more than one customer. When you have finished this exercise, you will have a clearer picture of who your customers are and what aspects of your products they deem most important.

Marketing Personas

Visualize three or more typical, but different, buyers of your product. Give each a name. Use your imagination. Form a mental picture of each person. Each should be representative of the type of person who will buy from you.

Some customers are worth more than others. When you find someone eager to talk about what you do, give her something to talk about. You probably serve many people, but profit from only a few. Customers come in all sizes and shapes. Your largest customers may require special handling. Whales pay for minnows.

List distinguishing personal characteristics for each person you've visualized. Consider character, wealth, attitude, education, age, hobbies, and dreams. Don't let your ideas about one person influence your description of the others. To make this easier, cover the other columns as you work on the characteristics of each customer.

It will be relatively easy to list the first three or four characteristics for each customer. But the next few will require some deeper thinking. Make that extra effort, because what really motivates people to buy usually comes from down deep, is not so obvious and almost always is personal.

Consider at least three types of customers. Make a list headed by each person's descriptive name (like Cautious Cal, Thrifty Ted, or Big Bucks Ben). Create enough of these to represent most of your customers. For each of these fictional human beings create a persona which includes the person's name, title and:

- **Location**
- **Demographics**—Factors such age, sex, race, religion, education, marital status, and income contribute to the picture. The Nielsen Claritas PRIZM system is available

online; it organizes demographic data into 66 distinct subsegments. Go to www.claritas.com.

- **Psychographics**—Lifestyle, behavioral and purchasing patterns, feelings, beliefs, values, and attitudes all contribute to a psychographic profile. People buy feelings, not things, because they want to fit in, gain status or otherwise take action that either helps them increase a sense of belonging or differentiating. This is a core concept in the book *Get People to Do What You Want*, by Gregory Hartley and Maryann Karinch.
- **Geodemographics**—In a way, this is a combination of all three – location, demographics, and psychographics. Also called cluster marketing and lifestyle marketing, it relies on various methods of classifying and characterizing neighborhoods or other well-defined areas based on the theory that residents living near each other will probably have similar demographic, socio-economic and lifestyle characteristics. The guiding principle is "birds of a feather flock together."

Common Characteristics

Compare the lists and circle the characteristics your customers have in common. What are the common denominators—the unifying characteristics? What do they have in common that would:

- Enable you to communicate with them easily?
- Describe and categorize them in something like Myers-Briggs terms? For example, they might be logicians, meaning they are analytical and intensely curious, or perhaps debaters, who are also very curious, but instinctively challenge your assertions and conclusions at every turn.
- Provide them the time and means to shop and compare?
- Require them to be cost conscious?

- Require them to act quickly?

Use your answers to create a composite picture of your typical customer. This is the person you will be thinking about when you create your sales pitches and marketing materials. Be able to give definitive answers to these key questions:

- What problems do they share?
- What benefits do most of them seek?

How, Where, When

How or where do customers prefer to purchase products like yours? How and where do they purchase your competitor's products? Is there an opportunity for you to make your product more convenient to purchase?

When is the best time to connect with your target customers? Certain times are better than others to make a sale. Determine when your prospects buy, whether it's a day of the week, a month of the year, or a season of the year. When are they most likely to purchase? What can you do to make it more convenient for them to buy at the optimum time? Can you extend this to other times of the year?

The Federal Government, for example, closes its fiscal year on September 30. During the month of September, they spend all the funds they didn't spend during the previous eleven months. Consequently, more government sales are made during that last week of September than any other week of the year. There are also obvious consumer purchases related to holidays, vacations, and the school year.

Wrap Up

- Create at least three personas. What are the most common uses/benefits amongst them?
- Describe your ideal prospect in detail.

Chapter 6: Positioning

Fashion fades: style is forever.

- Yves Saint Laurent
French Fashion Designer

Unless you are in the earliest phase of starting your company, your product and company already have a position in the minds of your prospective customers. When they hear your name, they already have an opinion on who you are and what you have to offer. That's your *position*. It's present tense. It's how your business is viewed by others today.

Positioning is different. It involves the future tense. Positioning is how you wish to be perceived in the days to come.

It needs to be attainable and relevant. It should both differentiate you from your competition and be independent of today's specific product offerings. In other words, positioning should be external to the product, independent of time, and non-perishable. This way, the perception can stay constant. Intangible factors like quality, service, or technological leadership can be very effective and will almost certainly last longer than product attributes.

When publishers think of a book like this one in terms of positioning, they see it in context. Knowing who the prime target market comprises, publishers ask themselves, "What else are these people buying and why?" This book held appeal to the publisher because it has a no-nonsense, no-frills approach to imparting practical business information for anyone selling something. It doesn't compete with business theory books, or books on business ethics, for example. The positioning is "a how-to book for entrepreneurs with no time to waste."

"If you can't fix it, feature it" was the great advice a restaurant owner friend of mine received when faced with an excessive rise in his food costs. Since he couldn't do much about it, instead he raised prices and repositioned his restaurant by featuring the most expensive and finest hamburger in town.

Go back and look at how your major competitors are positioned. Unless you have large sums of money to finance your battle for the buyer's mind, avoid taking a position like your competition. Position your company, not as better but different. You won't win with imitation. You win through differentiation and solving new problems.

The number one form of differentiation in any industry... is being number one!

- Marc Andreessen
Venture Capital, Financial Advisor

Wrap Up

What do you want people to think about when they hear your name?

Chapter 7: Your Story

Instead of focusing on what you're selling, instead tell a story of why you did it.

- Seth Godin
Author, *This Is Marketing*

Stories appeal to customer emotions. Great stories build trust between buyer and seller and help you connect emotionally with your customer. Your story should link what's important to the customer with your product.

Stories work because instead of drilling down on your products features and benefits and making customers think, stories plant memorable ideas and relationships in the customer's mind. Great stories do not appeal to logic; they appeal to the senses. Logic causes people to think; emotions cause people to act.

Your story must be based on truth and obviously have something to do with your prospect's pain point. It often involves a third-party and how a customer benefited from doing business with you (therefore endorsing your product). Your story and claims need to targeted and specific.

Find yours and tell it well. Make it brief. Then make it briefer. Here are some ideas for building a story.

- Identify current objections and how you resolved them.

- Tell about a customer who had trouble with your price and how it had a happy ending.
- Share how the product or your company came into existence.
- Identify quirky problems your product solves.
- Offer a surprise success story.
- Elaborate on what makes you different from the competition.

In *Sell with a Story*, bestselling author Paul Smith offers ten of the most compelling reasons for telling a sales story:

1. Stories help the buyer relax and just listen.
2. Stories help build strong relationships.
3. Storytelling speaks to the part of the brain where decisions are made.
4. Stories make it easier for the buyer to remember you, your ideas, and your product.
5. Storytelling increases the value of the product you're selling.
6. Storytelling highlights your main idea by moving it to another context.
7. Stories are contagious.
8. Storytelling gives you an opportunity to be original.
9. Your buyers want more stories from you.
10. Storytelling is more fun than delivering a canned sales pitch, for you and the buyer.

- Paul Smith, *Sell with a Story: How to Capture Attention, Build Trust, and Close the Sale*
(New York: AMACOM, 2016), pp 16-23

Wrap Up

What's your story?

Chapter 8: Competition

Buyers commonly do comparison shopping and Internet savvy buyers go out of their way to comparison shop. They know all about your competition and will expect you to tell them, and possibly prove, why you're the best choice. So, you'd better know what your competitors are saying.

If any of your competitors are public companies, send for their annual report and quarterly financial statements. If you buy a few shares of their stock, you'll be privy to all kinds of information.

If you are in a complex competitive environment and have the necessary staff, designate different people as specialists on each competitor (in addition to their regular jobs). Each is responsible for knowing all about a competitor and should maintain a complete file on the company and its products. Pull the findings together and create a reservoir of vital information on these areas:

- **Competitive positioning.** Advertising professionals claim that if you win the battle for mind share, market share will follow. Positioning a company means getting people to think about it in a specific way. Federal Express advertises: "Guaranteed delivery by 10 a.m. the next day."
- **What your competitors say they do best.** What do all your competitors claim that makes them different and best? What is their unique selling proposition? What evidence do they use? Is it true or are they exaggerating? Is it relevant? Are they consistent? How do you respond?

- **Reasons you lose to a competitor.** Look for common reasons why you lose business to competitors. When you lose to a specific competitor, do you usually lose for the same reasons? Do the reasons go beyond the product, for example, service, channel, convenience? If you were a competitor, how would you sell against you?
- **Objections.** You need to be prepared to handle objections. How will you respond to the prospect that seems to want exactly what the competition promises? When this happens, be assured your competitor's salesperson has converted that prospect to his way of thinking. Your job is to turn the tables around and get that person to now want what you have. For starters, you need pat answers for the first-level objections that you'll hear repeatably, such as price, delivery, availability, reliability, customer service, and terms and conditions.
- **Competitor Sales Channels.** The best sales channels put your product in the right place at the right time. Which sales channels provide your competitors with the most sales and profits?

Wrap Up

- What does each competitor do best?
- When a competitor beats you, why?
- What are you doing about that?

Chapter 9: Rolling Out Something New

Figure out what prospective customers are going to want before they do.

- Steve Jobs
Founder, Apple Computer

New products should attract attention for your company.

New winning products (including variations on existing products) are the lifeblood of any growth business. The challenge, of course, is not just to create something new, but also to create something people want to buy. Conformity is not a good idea. You really need to distinguish your product and differentiate it in the mind of the customer.

In Robert Heller's *The Supermarketers*, he wryly noted:

Creating new products is easy. All you must do is predict the future, understand new emerging customer needs, and satisfy those needs with clearly superior new products, quickly, before the competition does, at the highest possible levels of quality, for the lowest cost possible. Nothing to it.

- Robert Heller, *The Supermarketers: Marketing for Success, Rules of the Master Marketers, the Naked Marketplace*
(New York, Dutton, 1987)

Anything is possible

A few years ago, I was associated with a hardware start-up technology company that was just beginning to make serious sales. Their prospects were good, but early orders and revenues were growing slowly and, with luck—actually, with lots of luck—they might have come close to $3 million in sales that year.

Then, opportunity struck. Their president met with the marketing executive of a substantial Fortune 100 prospect who told him that if his start-up firm would custom-design and manufacture a special system for them, the customer would commit to $30 million in purchases over the next twelve months. However, the new systems would have to be designed and ready for production in ninety days.

Problem: The start-up's engineering staff estimated the work would take twelve months, not three. The president then made a presidential decision. He called the engineering manager and his four-man team into his office and made them an offer. If they could meet the deadline, he would give each of them a stock option that would likely be worth $1 million if the company's revenues increased ten-fold, to $30 million, in the coming year.

He then told the engineering manager to make a list, without considering cost, of everything he would need to make the 90-day deadline. The engineering manager did and came back with the ultimate wish list. It included a private facility in the Santa Cruz, CA mountains, away from corporate headquarters, over $200,000 worth of new equipment and software, subcontractor arrangements for another $100,000, and so on.

The president then went to his venture capital investors, got the $500,000 and granted all their wishes. One year later they all made a million dollars. Nothing is impossible.

Getting into the product business

There are several ways to get into the product business.

- Make it yourself. Especially in the beginning. This way you can test your idea before spending real money.
- Work with a manufacturing partner. You're going to have to commit to a minimum order size.
- Wholesale. If you can buy what you want to sell, do it. Margins will suffer, but this is usually a great first step.
- Dropship. Your gross margins will drop significantly, buy you avoid carrying inventory. If you do this, arrange where you get the customer's contact data.

Product leadership

What do your prospective customers value the most? What do the market leaders offer that has enabled them to rise to the top? Where is the market going? What do you estimate customers will value more in the future?

Consider several options for wedging your way into a more prominent position in the marketplace and protecting your interests so you stay there.

- **Knockoffs.** One fast and proven path to coming up with a new product is to identify a competitor's product and make a better or cheaper one. Add a feature, bundle in some services, lower the price, add a new distribution channel, give it more visual appeal, change the messaging. Examine competitive products to ascertain if there is one you could improve upon and take market share away from that competitor. What would you do to make customers switch from them to you?
- **Refurbishing old products.** Determine if you can re-vitalize your existing products—adding features, expanding value, lowering the cost/price, narrowing/broadening markets. Disruptive innovation is a term used when an existing product is so dramatically improved that it changes industry

norms and customer expectations. How can you enhance the value and competitiveness of your existing products?

- **Brand new products.** Think first about new products for your existing markets before you consider new products for new markets. Radically new products have turned many a poor company into a rich one. But be careful. Even if it is obviously a break-through idea, people tend to change more slowly than you may like. Help your customers understand the new by relating it to the old. Aside from the so-called early adopters, most people will wait till your innovative new product has made it to the mainstream. Not all new products need to be dramatically different. Customers may find changes in old familiar products more digestible. Sometime the changes can be in marketing, for example, during difficult economic times, advertising your more affordable items can keep the cash register going.
- **Optimizing your resources.** Don't make what you can buy. The NIH (Not Invented Here) syndrome plagues many companies. If something like the product you are thinking about already exists, consider becoming a reseller of it. Could you have it private-labeled or enter a joint marketing venture? You'll save development dollars and get to market a lot faster. Don't waste precious time and money going sideways or backwards. If the product you're thinking about doesn't already exist, however, look for someone who will make it for you for less money and/or faster than you can. Consider alternatives to using your own product development resources for new products.
- **Timing.** Being a first mover and getting into the market first, or at least early, is a powerful advantage. Plot ways to shorten the development process and/or time to market if possible. What about first releasing an abbreviated version? This approach has the added advantage of testing customer reactions before you make a full investment. In

many instances, you're better off getting to market with something that solves the customer's basic problem, even if it doesn't have all the bells and whistles you would like to include. In India, they use a product development method called jugaad (pronounced joo-gaardh) which is driven by the nation's scarce resources and the immediate needs (not wants) of their immense, hungry, and ready-to-buy-now population. This results in simpler products that are easy to make, deliver and support.

- **Protecting your idea and product.** Launching a new product can have legal ramifications. Laws in many countries do not necessarily protect "mere ideas" although non-disclosure or confidentiality agreements do help protect your idea from being pilfered. Often the best protection against the competition stealing your idea is to act fast. Once your idea becomes a product, with a name and specifications, it's easier to protect it legally. Know specifically how you will protect your idea from being copied by a competitor. When discussing your new product with another businessperson, it's prudent to use an NDA (Non-disclosure agreement) which is a legal contract between at least two parties to protect confidential material, knowledge, or privileged information.
- **Naming.** This is another potential legal minefield. As soon as possible, make a list of possible names and conduct a name search for each. These searches tend to be relatively inexpensive (a few hundred dollars) and cover registered trademarks in the appropriate classes, directories, and other places that might list competitors' marks. Too many companies skip this step only to later face re-branding expenses because they assumed a name was available. As a corollary, make sure customers will be able to find your product name on the web. Use similar care when choosing your website's URL.

More about naming. People notice and remember unusual names. Try to keep yours short. Record it to hear how the name will sound to others. Try it out in print, in both large and small fonts. Make it easy to spell and spell it like it sounds so that people can find you on the web or in the phone book. Would someone know the nature of the product by the name alone? Avoid acronyms. Too many downsides. Here is a humorous look at why from Phil Davis, Branding and Naming Expert and President of Tungsten Branding (tungstenbranding.com):

Here are the reasons abbreviations (not necessarily acronyms) make for poor brand names and sit near the top of the list of company naming mistakes:

- You will compete with every other company, in and out of your industry, that shares your letters (WWF... Wrestlers or Pandas?)
- You suffer dilution whenever a new company, or world event, impinges on your names (Can you say ISIS?)
- You must instill the brand message & values into an otherwise meaningless set of initials. (JQZY... the one name you can trust!)
- The pronunciation can present an issue even in shortened form (Did you say BMN Capital or VNM Capital or was it BNM?)
- The initials can present unwelcome meaning (Probably not smart to shorten Furman University) Or use initials such as BO, PU and WTF
- You miss the golden opportunity to differentiate your brand or point to a key value proposition (e.g. Take the voyage with Voya)
- You miss the opportunity to create "white space" around your company name, so potential customers find only you when they search.

- Phil Davis, "Company naming mistakes: Why abbreviations don't say much," https://www.tungstenbranding.com/2015/07/23/company-naming-mistakes/

Wrap Up

- What products/benefits are not now available from the leaders or anyone else?
- What products/benefits are customers going to want in the future?
- What can you do to get a head start on all this?

MARKETS

Chapter 10: Markets

There is only one winning strategy. It is to carefully define the target market and direct a superior offering to that market.

- Philip Kotler
Professor Emeritus of Marketing
Kellogg School of Management, Northwestern University

The late Gary Halbert, one of the world's greatest marketers, when teaching a class on marketing liked to test his students by challenging them to come up with a marketing plan for a hamburger stand. He tells them they are free to have anything they want for their stand.

The classes came up with lists: best meat, best location, best buns, condiments, best prices, and more.

Gary listened and commented, "Yes, you all do need some marketing training, because I could put together a hamburger stand that would outsell yours easily and all I would need is one thing."

"What's that?" they asked.

"A starving crowd," he answered.

- *The Gary Halbert Letter*
Cherrywood Publishing
Ocala, FL 34474

Target markets

Narrow your focus and broaden your reach.

When you solve a unique problem, you start to realize the benefits of a monopoly.

- Peter Thiel
Author, *Zero to One*

The idea here is to develop a reputation in your target market that makes you the first company people think about when they are shopping for products like yours. Beware of the deadly middle, where you're not the cheapest, not the highest quality, and worse yet not noticeably different.

You are not in the business of looking for marketing challenges, but rather looking for markets in which your chances of winning are the greatest and the competition is the weakest.

Factors to consider include:

- Demand. Which markets are growing?
- Softest targets. Where is the competition least entrenched?
- Time. Which markets can you get to fastest?
- Customer satisfaction. Where are you most likely to make customers the happiest?
- Cost. In which markets are your costs the lowest?

The overarching question is this: Where do you have the best chance of winning (or not losing)? You must identify where the competitor's heavy artillery is not yet in place or doesn't mean much with these buyers.

The smaller, the better

Until you're the market leader, be very selective when venturing into markets where the demand bell curve is peaking, that is, avoid mature markets. Instead look up front where customer's emerging new needs are not yet being met and where serious competitors don't pay a lot of attention. Start with a group that's reachable. The smaller the better. Early adopters are perfect since they can tolerate incomplete offerings and the absence of reference accounts.

Non-disruptive marketing

We tend to think that to gain market share we need to disrupt the status quo and replace the market leader with something better. In most cases that will be impractical and likely impossible. A far more practical and achievable approach is to 1) think small and identify a customer need that is not being well satisfied by the market leader and then 2) position your company and product as specialists solving those very problems. What you're doing is creating a market segment in which you'll become the leader.

Market segmentation

Segment your total market into individual, homogeneous groups. Use common industry descriptions, like the North American Industry Classification System (NAICS) codes or market definitions used by market research firms to segment your market(s). This way you can find and use market research data that probably already exists. Someone has most likely put significant time and energy into sizing, segmenting, and projecting your market. Use their data and market definitions because:

You make it doubly hard to entice people to invest in or write about your firm if they first must learn about your business and markets. Describe your business so that anyone can understand what you do. Selling and marketing is tough enough. Don't compound your problem by using terminology people don't understand.

Logistics

Location

In zeroing in on your target market(s) you need to know where they are if physical location is a factor and how to reach them. If you need a physical location, myriad sources of satellite data will direct your further research related to language, traffic, and climate, for example.

Special market knowledge

You and your competitors have people, equipment, and money. However, there is always one difference between you and them—what you know that they don't. Using that to reach customers is a logistical triumph.

Sales Channels

You probably have two kinds of customers. One is your sales channel, which can include Channel Partners, Distributors, and Retailers who resell your products to the end users. The second is your end customers—the users of the products.

Before you worry about end customers, make certain your sales channels are sold on you. If they aren't enthusiastic, you don't have a chance. Salespeople and resellers want products that:

- Serve markets they already know
- Customers have heard about
- Sell easily
- Are delivered on time
- Stimulate repeat sales

Credibility

Customers like products recommended by others. They also like to buy products from companies they trust. So, customer credibility is a major issue. Customers should know who you are and believe in you.

If you are going after a market where customers already know you, then you have some credibility. If, however, you are entering a new market, then you will have to do something that may be expensive and time consuming (like advertising) to make sure strangers learn about you.

Consider customer credibility from a product and market point of view, that is, from a Current/New product and a Current/New Market perspective.

- Product: A Current Product is now on sale. A New Product has never been sold before.
- Market: A Current Market is one in which you participate and are known. A New Market is one where customers are unaware of you or your products.

This results in four scenarios. The lesson here is in the fourth quadrant. Companies trying to sell new products to people who never heard of them or their products, soon discover it takes much more time than planned. It takes time to become credible. This is a major reason why most new ventures fail.

<table>
<tr><td colspan="4">Current Product – Now being sold</td></tr>
<tr><td rowspan="2">Current Market – Customers know who you are</td><td>1. Lowest risk. Customers know you and your product</td><td>2. Takes time and money to make customers in a new market aware of you</td><td rowspan="2">New Market – Customers never heard of you</td></tr>
<tr><td>3. At least the customers know you. This is where most new ventures succeed.</td><td>4. Highest risk. A new, unproven product into a market that's never heard of it or your firm</td></tr>
<tr><td colspan="4">New Product – Never been sold</td></tr>
<tr><td colspan="4">Current and New Product/Market Matrix</td></tr>
</table>

Not all markets are created equal

If you have multiple markets in mind, choose the one where the market is in its earliest stages, where the competition is the weakest, and you or someone around you has experience in and around the market. Concentrate your resources.

Take advantage of free market data from websites such as census.gov/quickfacts and https: www.statcan.gc.ca/eng/start.

You could also try survey services such as surveymonkey.com. In addition, check out the free keyword research tools like wordtracker.com and search insight tools such as www.answerthepublic.com

You can search incognito with the Google Chrome web browser to get cleaner results from Google since they won't be affected by the search engines ability to track your search history.

Covering all the bases

According to studies, there are between three to six people involved in a typical industrial buying decision; yet less than half of these people ever meet the "winning" salesperson.

From this, you could conclude that since the salespeople aren't selling, many products are bought, rather than sold. Certainly, some of the blame must go to the salesperson for not doing a thorough job. But let's face it, all salespeople have limited time.

That's why you need companion marketing promotions with a broader reach to augment and complement your direct salespeople's selling activities. Advertising, public relations campaigns, direct mail, and telemarketing do wonders for awareness and make cold calls easier and more effective. Your objective is to inform those "other people" who never do meet your salesperson, that the company and product your company is considering is coming from a reputable source.

Let your marketing programs handle the influencers (people whose opinions affect the buying decision). Use your high-powered, high-priced salespeople for the critical calls in the target accounts with the most qualified prospects.

Wrap Up

- What do you know about the market that is special and important to the customer?
- What will it take to for you to become a market leader?

Chapter 11: Government

A giant market with small business set asides—that's how those of us who have done business with a government see it.

It can be daunting to do business with an enormous entity such as the federal government of the United States. But many a business has gone from zero to millions by doing their homework, filling out the right forms, getting the right credentials, and selling to subcontractors or directly to government agencies. In fact, even individual consultants can do regular business with the government by just filling out the paperwork correctly and having the skills a government agency requires.

US Government Goals

As of this writing, 23 percent of federal contract dollars go to small business and it typically reaches that goal. In 2018, 23.88 percent of federal contract dollars went to small business, totaling $105.87 billion. The Department of Defense (DOD) spends the most money (about 70 percent of all procurements); the rest is spent by civilian agencies like the Department of Commerce, Treasury, and Agriculture.

To get started, you first need to enroll and create a User Account in the System for Award Management (SAM) e-procurement system. This will register you to do business with the US government.

You should also register with the Government Services Administration (GSA). By doing so, you will qualify with many state and local governments who honor the federal schedules.

And you should also register on the Federal Business Opportunities web site (www.fbo.gov/). This site publishes all contract opportunities worth more than $25,000.

Federal Acquisition Regulations (FARs) define procurement rules. If you're really going to do lots of government contract bidding, you probably ought to hire a consultant to help you out—especially in the beginning.

Selling to a prime contractor instead of directly to the government is often the most efficient way to go in reaping the benefits of government contracts. Doing business as a subcontractor to companies that act as prime contractors is a great way to leverage their marketing and infrastructure investments. For contracts over $550,000, prime contractors must provide the government with an acceptable plan to subcontract some of the work to small business or be considered ineligible for the contract. Subcontracting opportunities can be found at www.gsa.gov/subdirectory.

"Disadvantaged" businesses have real advantages as well. Some classes of disadvantaged small businesses are treated specially. This sometimes extends to the point that they receive sole-source contracts, qualify for limited competition contracts, or can win contracts when their bids are up to 10 percent higher than the low bidder.

Disabled veteran-owned businesses, for example, may qualify. A disadvantaged (for example, certain ethnicities and small net worth) small business owner whose company has been in business for less than two years may qualify for the 8(a) Business Development Program. There is even a HUBZone Program for small businesses with a significant percentage of their employees living in designated low-income or underutilized areas.

Science and technology companies have special paths to sources of development funding as well. The Small Business Innovative Research (SBIR) and Small Business Technology Transfer (STTR) award grants, and Broad Agency Announcements (BAAs) provide routes to government contracts. SBIR and STTR are known as America's Seed FundÔ; startups in many other countries have similar opportunities.

The SBIR program is designed to help meet federal research and development needs; its goal is to fund innovations with commercial potential. A highly competitive program, it is supposed to allow special concessions for women and socially or economically disadvantaged people. The STTR program includes joint ventures between small businesses and not-for-profit research institutions. STTR aims to bridge the gap between performance of basic science and commercializing the innovations that result. BAAs involve scientific or research projects and some early-stage development efforts. They are notices published online at the Federal Business Opportunities (FedBizOpps.gov) website and proposals from private firms of any size are welcomed. Proposals through BAA are peer reviewed or go through a similar vetting process.

Ongoing Opportunity

Doing business with the government is good business. Not too many years ago, companies doing government business were looked upon unfavorably; especially by the Wall Street types who cited low margins, slow growth, and long sales cycles. Today, those opinions have changed. The Federal Government is one sector of the economy that's always growing and shows no signs of slowing down. Further, they are mandated to help small business and they always pay their bills. All this makes the Federal Government a hard market to ignore. Identify local, state, or federal agencies where you think your products might fit. Then:

- Do a little research and document how the agency would benefit by doing business with you.

- Call their contracts personnel. Find out what it takes to get on their qualified vendor list and who in their agency you should be talking to.
- Make an appointment to meet with someone who can brief you beyond what websites offer.
- Do the same thing with some of the agency's potential prime contractors.

Wrap Up

- Contact the appropriate government agencies, make friends, and follow their directions.

Chapter 12: Going International

One way for US-based companies to simplify doing business outside of the United States is selling through distributors. International distributors are commonly more resourceful than their American counterparts and are used to dealing with long supply lines and distant support.

Alternatively, consider Alibaba.com to sell to foreign resellers and end users without ever getting on an airplane. In 2019, Alibaba opened to US sellers, and that opportunity is explored in greater depth later in the book.

Different Levels of Involvement

There are three primary strategies for international marketing through distributors:

- Casual. Fulfill unsolicited foreign orders through an export agent.
- Active. Sign up foreign distributors to sell your existing product line without making significant changes in your products or market strategy.
- Customized. Create localized products and promotions for each international market according to cultural, regional, and national differences. You adapt your existing products for each market, invent new ones, or simply adjust your

promotions for each market. Changing the marketing is more common and costs less than changing the product.

Globalization

You can treat the whole world as one market and ignore regional and national differences. In other words, you can sell standard products (usually with some minor modifications) everywhere using similar marketing promotions, pricing, and distribution. This is the strategy used by some manufacturers of computer equipment, soft drinks, and athletic shoes, and by fast foods companies like Pizza Hut and Kentucky Fried Chicken.

International Representation

Establishing an international presence may appear daunting, but it only takes a little initiative and follow-up.

One business owner got started by identifying English-language magazines that covered his industry in the countries where he sought representation. He then leafed through each magazine and identified companies and people who looked like they might be interested in either representing his firm or buying his products.

Next, he contacted each, announcing what he was looking for. Out of the few hundred emails sent, he got back close to a hundred responses. Responders received a second email announcing his planned visit and requested detailed information on the respondent's businesses. That in turn provided him with enough information to set up an agenda, prioritize his appointments, and turn his first international trip into a success.

National/Regional Differences

Even though the US market is really thousands of regional markets, from a big picture point of view, it is quite homogenous compared to international markets. From language to cultural differences, there is far more parochialism between international countries.

The Pacific Rim nations, Western Europe, Eastern Europe, North America, and South America are the primary international market sectors.

Treaties in which the United States participates—like the WTO (World Trade Organization and USMCA (United States-Mexico-Canada Agreement)—tend to promote international trade. So do other factors, such as Most Favored Nation (MFN) status, which describes a reciprocal bilateral relationship between countries that decide to give each other certain trading privileges.

No matter what your international strategy, you will probably have to make some product or marketing program modifications. For example, McDonald's restaurants in Saudi Arabia close four times a day for 30 to 40 minutes to accommodate Muslim prayer traditions.

Local, influential forces shape each international market:

- Cultural—Concepts, values, buildings, foods that make up a society
- Social—Family, religion, education, health, and recreation
- Economic—Standards of living, availability of credit, disposable income, income distribution
- Political—National laws, tariffs, payoffs, red tape
- Technological—Availability of services. Direct mail, on-line, radio, and television advertising don't work in countries that lack up-to-date Internet, broadcast, and postal services.
- Distribution—getting to the customer

If you sell services, you'll probably have to develop your own distribution channels or perhaps enter a strategic alliance (to save the costs of going it alone) with an indigenous firm serving the same customers.

If you have products that need to be explained and serviced, you'll need to have a close, hands-on relationship with your international resellers. If you sell something like toys, then you will be more involved with agents and wholesalers. Or you can make Original Equipment Manufacturer (OEM) arrangements with US manufacturers already targeting your international markets. There are several typical strategies for developing distribution channels, including:

- **Exporting.** This is the lowest level of international selling and the most flexible. Export agents bring buyer and seller together and collect a commission for arranging the sale. Export houses and export merchants purchase products from different companies and sell them to foreign companies.
- **Direct Ownership**. At the other end of the commitment spectrum is a company that makes a long-term investment by funding and starting a subsidiary or division in the foreign country. This may include manufacturing and distribution and can be very expensive.
- **Licensing.** This is a much lower-cost alternative to direct ownership. The licensee is the owner of a foreign operation that typically manufactures and sells a product that has already been successful domestically. The licensee pays an initial fee and then pays commissions back to the licensor for every product sold. The licensor provides management and technical assistance along with a successful product. If you choose this approach, you're relying on the licensee's bookkeeping. You might be better off with a fixed fee arrangement.
- **Joint Ventures.** These are partnerships between a domestic firm and a foreign firm or government. Control varies with the arrangement. Joint ventures are often the best way to do business in countries in which nationalism is strong or where consolidation of resources is necessary.
- **Strategic Alliance.** This is like a joint venture. Usually the partners retain their distinct identities but share common long-term business goals.

- **Trading Companies.** As their name implies, trading companies are not manufacturers; they buy products in one country and sell them in another. They take title to the products and are responsible for all the costs in selling and transporting them to buyers.

Online Venues

When you offer your products for sale on both Amazon.com and Ebay.com, your US listings can also be made accessible to international buyers. In these cases, Amazon, and eBay handle most of the logistics.

Alibaba.com is a business to business sales (B2B) venue now available to US sellers. Here, the transaction is between the seller and buyer only and the logistics are worked out by the two parties. Alibaba simply provides vendors with exposure (like a trade show) gives buyers a place to find companies and products they might want to buy.

Pricing

Pricing can be tricky, especially when you start thinking about how much margin you'll need from international sales.

Most companies use a cost-plus approach to pricing, that is, they simply add the incremental costs of international taxes, transportation, and any special handling to the cost of the product, and then price the offering to produce margins comparable to a domestic sale. This means your international operations are paying their fair share (or at least some portion) of your business's overhead, but it will cause your international prices to be higher than domestic prices.

Some companies sell their products for about the same price as in the United States (resulting, of course, in reduced gross margin) and use their domestic operations to pay for the bulk of their overhead. Some carry this to an illegal extreme (called dumping) and price their products for the international markets below the prices they charge domestically.

Prices are also affected by foreign currency exchange rates. Fluctuation in the value of currency will affects markups and prices charged to international customers.

Payment can be in US dollars or in foreign currency. Historically, when American companies chose to be paid in US dollars, they faced possible delays due to foreign exchange regulations abroad. The alternative was choosing to receive the payment in a foreign currency. That meant they assumed the risk of that currency dropping in value against the dollar and the added task of converting the foreign currency into US dollars.

These days, the computerized fund-transfer software some US banks employ allows international clients to pay in their own currency. This makes the client's life easier and the risks of foreign exchange rates are outweighed by the ease and speed of the operation.

Success tips

You will tend to over rely on your representative's knowledge of the territory because (1) that's why you hired them and (2) you don't want to take the time to learn it yourself. This is a good reason to initially concentrate on just a few countries. Doing so allows you to get first-hand knowledge of the opportunities and you don't have to rely on too many strangers (some of whom don't even work for you) for information.

Even if you're in a market where knowledge of English is common, translate your literature into the native language. If you have English-only literature, you are only communicating with a fraction of the market. And even those who understand English would rather read about your products in their native language.

Don't spend most of your advertising budget on the US market and then throw what's left over at the international markets.

The further you are away from home, the greater the advertising requirement—another good reason to concentrate on just a few foreign markets.

Finally, when you advertise remember that what's creative in the United States may be offensive or even stupid elsewhere. Forget the puns and the jokes, stick to the facts.

Substantive help on this front is available from a variety of sources. The US Small Business Administration's ELAN (Export Legal Assistance Network) can help you with tariffs, regulatory requirements, distributor agreements, export licenses, and so on. The US Commerce Department has a 24-hour service that features hard-to-get information on subjects like doing business in Russia. The International Business Development program at Northwestern University in Evanston, Illinois will help any American business owner interested in pursuing international business. And many state governments offer direct (and free) assistance to help you make the right contacts and find the right international partners.

Wrap Up

Find someone who has experience selling your kind of products internationally and let that expert mentor you.

DECISION MAKING

Chapter 13: Behavioral Economics

Time to apply psychological insights into human behavior to explain customers' decision making. Even when the decisions seem odd, you want to do everything possible to make them predictable.

Some market studies have shown that consumer decision making is less that 30 percent rational and as much as 70 percent emotional. Advertising and marketing, which try to shape how people think about their choices, thrive under these conditions.

Intuitive Decision Making

Decades ago, psychologists Amos Tversky and Daniel Kahneman published research papers on understanding the consumer psyche and the irrationality of the human's decision-making process. Their findings started a revolution in economics to the degree that Kahneman was awarded a Nobel Prize in Economic Sciences in 2002. (The Royal Swedish Academy of Sciences does not award prizes posthumously and Tversky had died in 1996.)

Their research, now called Behavioral Economics, debunked centuries-old conventional wisdom that assumes humans are rational and make reasonable decisions, specifically in this case, weighing costs against benefits to maximize value and profit. Their studies revealed that this mainstream thinking is false.

Research revealed that instead of robot-like logic, real people make decisions using all sorts of irrational, self-sabotaging, self-serving behavior. These studies reveal that when making decisions, emotions strongly influence normal humans and that just about all our judgements and predictions based on human intuition are wrong.

Older, mainstream theories depended on the idea that "rational man" is an intelligent, analytical, selfish creature with perfect self-regulation in pursuit of his future goals and is immune to bodily states and feelings. And that he assumes a direct relationship between the buyer's choice and the object. Consequently, if the seller produces a better product, the market will price it correctly, and the resulting transaction will maximize both the buyer's and seller's interests.

We know now this is not how it happens. Instead, "normal man's" choice depends on how he sees the object, that is, people do not choose between things, they choose between descriptions of things.

The Framing of Decisions and Choice

The frame a decision maker adopts is controlled partly by the formulation of the problem (how it is presented/packaged) and partly by the norms, habits, and characteristics of the decision maker.

Advertising frames the choice so that it skews the choice in favor of the seller. Done correctly, the advertiser will have played on the buyer's emotions and can cause the buyer to purchase something he doesn't really need, buy more than necessary, and/or pay a higher price.

Heuristics and Human Bias

We study natural stupidity instead of artificial intelligence.

- Amos Tversky

From behavioral economics many ideas have emerged that tend to explain how and why people make decisions based more on intuition than actual logic. Understanding these biases can be an invaluable aid in crafting effective sales and marketing messages that go beyond the classic reasons for buying, that is, feature, function, and benefits.

Heuristics (from the Greek word for discover) describes problem solving techniques. Think of heuristic as a simple rule or procedure someone goes through to decide something.

Heuristics and all human biases provide us with insight on the human decision-making process. Here are some of our intuitive heuristics and resultant biases people use to make judgements and decisions. Exploit them in your advertising campaigns.

NOTE: Much of the following list is not original work and has been gathered from publicly available sources.

Positioning/Presentation

Representative	Here people compare whatever they are judging to some model in their mind. For example, when evaluating a person for a job, people tend to look for a stereotype who has some of the same characteristics of a person already doing that type of job successfully. How similar is A to B? If A looks like or has characteristics like B, who has performed spectacularly, then your intuition tells you A is a good choice.
Anchoring	Allowing initial information to have a disproportionate impact on our decisions. Consumers rely heavily on first impressions and use it as a benchmark for subsequent decisions. For example, your line of winter coats is priced at $499 and up and then you mark one style down to $99, creating the effect that an expensive coat is now a great buy.

Choice Overload	Shoppers were given a choice of twenty-four jams and another similar group was given a choice of six. The larger number drew a bigger crowd than the smaller one, but few made a purchase. Fewer shoppers stopped to taste the six jams, however sales from that group were more than five times higher than when presented with twenty-four.
Default Option	Defaults are what you get if you don't actively make a choice. When we are given something by default, it becomes more valuable than it would be otherwise—and we are more loath to part with it. Further, default does not require any further action on the part of the recipient—and doing nothing is a lot easier and more convenient than having to take an action.
Payment Pain	Delaying when payments start can dramatically increase sales
Inferior Options	By offering clearly inferior options (which will not sell) alongside what you really want to sell, you'll increase the better product's sales.
Loss Aversion	Consumers tend to believe it is worth taking risks to avoid the psychological pain from losing something you already have as opposed to the pleasure of a gain; for example, "Stop losing $100 per year with XYZ" works better than "Save $100 per year with XYZ."
Decoy Effect	Options influence customer decisions. Customers tend to buy the more expensive option when a third, less desirable option is offered.
Power of Free	Buy one get one free. Get 50 percent off if you buy two. Which one would you choose? We just love the word "free."

Irrational Value Psychology of Price	When asked to taste two bottles of identical wines, where one is marked with a price of $10 and the other for $45, the more expensive bottle gets a much higher rating. It turns out that we inherently believe that cheaper stuff offers inferior performance, that is, price is an indicator of quality.
Attribute Priming	By talking about a certain product feature, the seller can get the prospect to start thinking about that attribute which can ultimately affect their decision in favor of that feature. This is how you use specialization to get customers to want what you do best and therefore better than your competitors.
Salience	Being noticeable or important. Brand names for example can be used to infer quality. Visual salience occurs with a bold headline or having the sales price in a larger font than the regular price.
Metaphor	A metaphor is a figure of speech that describes an object or action in a way that isn't literally true. It can act as a substitute for thinking and replace genuine uncertainty, steering the reader or listener away from the truth. "My advice is an earthquake" is a metaphor. Note: If the sentence were, "My advice is like an earthquake", then the expression would be a simile, which also invites imagination to steer the reader or listener toward a feeling rather than a fact.
Social Proof	Word of mouth and online reviews all help convince prospects to become customers.

Human Nature

Present Bias	There is a strong sense of immediacy and undervaluing the future in relation to the present.
Status quo bias	We have a tendency for things to remain the same and not change behavior unless the incentive to do so is compelling.
Endowment Effect	Consumers tend to value items they own more than a similar one owned by someone else. Customization therefore increases emotional attachment.
Last Impressions	Last impressions can be lasting impressions.
Bounded Rationality	The rationality of a decision is based on information available, how smart the decision maker is, and the time available to make the decision.
Availability Heuristic	When faced with a decision, people may recall a recent, somewhat similar situation and have it affect their judgement.
Affect Heuristic	Judgement and decision making are often affected by good or bad feelings or biases that surface automatically when people think about a certain subject.
Temporal Dimensions	People are biased toward the present and poor predictors of future experiences, value perceptions and behavior, for example, most people will opt to receive $100 now instead of $110 a month from now.
Diversification Bias	Our present self is not good at predicting our future preferences, for example, if you go food shopping right after eating a big meal, your choices will not be optimal for later when you're particularly hungry.
Systematic Bias	People keep making the same mistakes, and they are predictable and systematic.

Confirmation Bias	Forming a near-instant opinion. People bring along a prejudice and are always looking to have that prejudice confirmed. We humans are not good at seeing things we did not expect to see and too eager to see what is expected.
Error	To acknowledge uncertainty is to admit the possibility of error.
Conditionality Heuristic	People no not incorporate into their estimates that conditions may drastically change.
Sample size	The smaller the sample size, the more likely it is to be unrepresentative of the wider population.
Halo Effect	If a person is judged generally great, he will be judged better than he really is.
Optimistic Future	When we plan, we are often wildly optimistic. We also regularly underestimate how long it is going to take to complete a task and tend to ignore experience.
Trust/Dishonesty	Trust can make us vulnerable. Dishonesty in human terms is a violation of trust. In business, dishonesty is not just about proposed gains and costs but also about self-deception like not declaring product deficiencies.
Fairness/ Reciprocity	Fairness is the human desire for reciprocity, our tendency to return another's action with another equivalent action. Reciprocity can be positive or negative. People's responses to positive actions are often kinder than necessary. Charities use reciprocity to their advantage by sending out donation letters offering larger gifts for higher donations.
Social Norms	Social norms signal appropriate behavior or actions taken by most of the people. For example, a charity informed potential donors that the typical member donation was $300, and the charity subsequently saw up to a 12 percent increase in average contribution size.

Simulation Heuristic	People simulate the future and then base their judgements and decisions in part on imagined scenarios.
Hindsight Bias	People overestimate the probability that a situation will turn out the way it has in the past.
Framing Effect	The framing effect is an example of cognitive bias, in which people react to a choice in different ways depending on how it is presented. You can present options in a positive frame—the option is surrounded by benefits—or in a negative frame—the option is seen as bordered by vicious beasts (that's a metaphor).
Choice Architecture	How choices are designed and presented to consumers, can dramatically impact the presentation and the consumer decision-making.
Optimism Bias	Largely inherited. Comes from a feeling of well-being. Plays a role on an individual's willingness to take a risk.

Analytic Data vs Subject Matter Experts

Behavioral economics has shown how we human beings fail to be rational in our judgements and predictions.

All of this has led to a general mistrust in human intuition and the frailties of human cognition. Consequently, there are significant movements to take the human opinion out of the decision making and prediction business and instead use hard data to weigh a situation with a deference to analytics, algorithms, and big data.

That makes sense. If human judgement is very biased, then you'd be well advised to use hard data rather than expert opinions. Whereas perfect answers don't exist, statistics can get you closer to a better answer than just relying on your present state of mind and intuition.

Knowledge is anything that increases your ability to forecast an outcome; in everything you do you're trying to predict the right thing.

Making Good Decisions

I, you, and everyone else fall into the behavioral economics web. We all regularly make decisions based on gut feel and intuition rather than on relevant facts. Here is what you can do about that.

Pay Attention

Good decision-making requires thought. Take a minute. No off- the-top-of your-head answers. With a one-second pause between question and answer, you're reacting, not thinking.

Do not let your mood and emotions get in the way of facts and figures. What else should I know that would help me make a better decision? Realize, you are never going to have all the information you want and need to make a fully informed decision. Therefore, in the absence of certainty, probability prevails. And probability has no memory; each new outcome is completely independent of the past. The only things certain are your thoughts and problem-solving processes. To get good at making decisions, you need to become comfortable with uncertainty.

There will be times when you do what's right, but the outcome is unfavorable. The cause is called bad luck and it happens to everyone. That's life. Focus on the process, not the luck. Put emotions and bad breaks aside. Luck is short term; skill prevails in the long term.

Although you cannot control the situation, you can control your attention, priorities, and what data you will consider. When others, especially opponents, are affected by your decision, consider how they will react. Don't worry about how your decision will affect how people think about you. As my old friend, minister and mentor, Terry Cole-Whittaker says, "What you think of me is none of my business."

Before you do act, ask yourself what's different now versus similar situations in the past. Knowledge is strength. The more you know, the better your judgement. When you are prepared to act, challenge yourself, questioning why this and not that. Pay attention.

Wrap Up

- Research reveals that rational decision-making is a rarity. Seventy five percent of all decisions are based on intuition and gut feel.
- People make decisions based on how they see the situation, that is, how it is framed and their personal desires such as gaining status or fitting in.
- When making your own decisions, take the time to consider facts and figures.
- Fast answers are almost always wrong.
- Don't let your emotional self, get in the way of your logical one.

MARKETNG COMMUNICATIONS

Chapter 14: MARCOM (Marketing Communications)

Before you choose how you are going to talk to your market (ads, media coverage, email, mail, YouTube videos), determine what you want to happen when people view your website, or read your articles, or see your ads. Objectives will likely vary by the medium.

- **Attitudes.** Are you trying to change what people currently think about your company or product? What are people's existing attitude about you? What attitude do you want people to have?
- **Awareness.** Do prospective customers even know who you are? What could you say or do, to get their attention and increase awareness? How will you stand out and make a good first impression?
- **Education.** Do you need to teach prospective customers about your technology, products, and approach? What do you need to teach them and what is the best way to do that: In person? With a video? Through an article or blog post?
- **Behavior**. What do you want prospects to do once they become aware of you? Make a purchase? Visit your store? Complete a request for information (lead) card? Exactly what do you want people to do after they hear about your product?

Sales messages

You have probably already composed a list of compelling reasons for people to buy your product, however, you may want to tweak them after you listen to your prospects and existing customers and hear how they express those compelling reasons. Sales messages should titillate people to take their next step to buy what you sell. You need to say what will make audiences pay attention, what makes you different.

The question here is "What?" not "How?" Leave creative strategy for another person or another day. You are not looking for headlines or visuals. You're looking for content. Don't settle for product features or functions. You want real customer benefits. Advertising agencies are usually very good at determining selling messages. Here's an example, from the computer industry, of how an advertising marketer might question a Client (the company selling the product) to uncover the real customer benefits:

Marketer: What's special about your new communications software product?

Client: It has data purity capability. *(Feature)*

Marketer: What does data purity do?

Client: It eliminates redundant information. *(Function)*

Marketer: What's so good about that?

Client: This shortens the time it takes to transmit a message. *(Benefit)*

Marketer: By how much?

Client: Approximately 25 percent. *(Quantification)*

Marketer: So, what? What does that mean to the customer?

Client: An annual savings of about $100 on their telephone bill *(Real Benefit)*.

Test your messaging

Show your message to a variety of people and ask them what they think. You'll get invaluable feedback. I have found the best feedback comes from people I call rocks, that is, the kind of people who have a palpable distaste for marketing and marketers in general. Their comments are usually insightful and if you can get them to give you an unenthusiastic nod, you probably have something that can work.

Some marketers claim that if your readers start to critique your message, you've probably got trouble and may have to rewrite it. They think that a correctly written message should stimulate and involve the reader so much that he or she will forget about critiquing and instead ask how to buy the product. In any case, getting lots of feedback is always a good idea.

Other audiences

Even if you communicate messages directly to consumers, remember to keep other relevant parties in the chain of communication informed, including intermediaries like resellers and third-party sales organizations. And don't forget the importance of reaching the eyes and ears of media, industry experts, and influential trade and professional associations.

If there is a reseller (retailer, distributor) between you and the consumer, then a ***push strategy*** is used to motivate the reseller to push and sell your product. ***A pull strategy*** is aimed at the consumer; it pulls consumers to your reseller or to you.

Most businesses use a combination of these strategies.

- Push works if the resellers do their job.
- Pull works if customers like what they see. Generally, pull works better than push.

If you are strapped for cash, choose a push strategy—because there are fewer of these and at least you know who your resellers are and how to reach them. See if you can work out some sort of co-op arrangement in which they spend some of their money needed for a corresponding pull strategy.

Marketing media

Marketing media are often categorized as passive or active, that is, passive where the audience has no direct involvement such as TV or radio; or active like reading or using a PC/smart phone where the viewer interacts with the delivery vehicle.

Direct marketing is action oriented and measurable. Brand marketing is culturally oriented and not measurable. In brand, you can't afford to be going after everyone. Be specific.

Interruptive vs permission marketing

- ***Interruptive marketing*** is the term for any marketing message or technique that consumers did not ask to receive. It includes direct mail, phone calls or text messaging that cuts into people's activities and redirects their attention. Interruptive can be capital intensive as it targets a wide audience with no guarantee of an acceptable return on investment (ROI).
- ***Permission-based marketing*** is customer-centered, allowing the customer to be an active part of the marketing communication—not just a passive recipient. Permission-based marketing costs less than interruptive marketing because the campaign is targeted and more measurable.

Action Plan

You'll need to choose your delivery media and methods to realize those marketing communications objectives. How are you going to contact your target audiences?

- **Medium:** Lots of choices here. Advertising, direct mail, e-mail, search engines, blogging, social media, public relations, articles, brochures, flyers, trade shows, webinars, seminars.

- **Objective:** Need to determine which is best for awareness, or to educate, or for lead generation or for making sales.
- **Marketing Calendar and Budget:** When is all this going happen and how much will it cost? To determine what is most important, consider what you would do if you only had half the amount you plan on spending. How much are you prepared to spend on each and what do you expect back and in what time frame?

Wrap Up

A few years ago, I co-authored a White Paper on marketing with Judy Rendich, President of BB&R Marketing, a major-league direct marketing company. Here is her advice to would-be direct marketers:

> *Repeat after me: as a marketer my sole purpose in life is to **identify** people who might have interest in what my company does, figure out how to put myself in **touch** with them, **understand** their needs, **offer** them good reasons to think about doing business with me, and **motivate** them to get off their butts and do what I am asking them to do.*

- What is your primary marketing communications objective?
- What are the media, budget, and time frame for your communications program?

Chapter 15: Advertising

Advertising attracts potential buyers, stimulates interest, and engenders positive feelings about your company. Good advertising causes people to think about you and your product at just the right time—when they start shopping for what you sell. Bad advertising goes unnoticed.

On the Internet there are numerous "free" advertising sites. Try them if they work, you save money. However most legitimate advertising costs money. As one of my advertisers once said, "I'm sure that only a small percentage of the ads we run work; I just wish I knew which ones." He was talking about awareness ads without a call to action. Advertisements, no matter how well constructed and properly placed, are commonly ignored, and don't usually work. Open a newspaper or a magazine—particularly a trade magazine—or go to the home page of a website like msn.com and glance at the ads. As the ads pass you by, ask yourself if it might cause a prospective buyer of that product to pause and read it.

See what I mean? Now don't get me wrong. You should advertise. Advertising can bring vitality to a business. But you need to be diligent, analytical, experimental, creative and, like it or not, you need to be patient.

Before you spend any money on advertising, read a good book on the subject. Try the classic *Ogilvy on Advertising*, which was written by David Ogilvy and published by Vintage Books in 1985, or one written more recently, like *Creative Advertising* by Mario Pricken (Thames & Hudson, 2008).

Radio, TV, and print were the mainstays of the advertising world for years. Advertising is more of a metaphor, whereas sales and marketing are more about results. Today's digital technology has changed some of that and put more power in the hands of the audiences. Nonetheless, advertising basics still prevail.

Differences between B2C and B2B Advertising

Retailers want as many people as possible to respond to their ads. That's because the retailer's selling costs are about the same no matter how many people respond to the ad and come into the store. It's also why they tend to advertise lots of items; they want to attract the largest crowd possible. The greater the response,, the greater their return on investment.

Business-to-business is different because the greater the response, the higher the cost of sales. That's because every respondent costs the advertiser money. At a minimum, the advertiser must capture the respondent's name, email more information, or mail some literature, and make a follow-up phone call. If the person making the follow-up call fails to qualify the respondent properly, a salesperson may spend hours traveling and meeting with people who can't possibly buy.

Therefore, B2B ads should be clear on what is being offered and stimulate prospects into action. This way you limit the number of respondents to those people with real interest in your product. In the world of business-to-business, unqualified leads, unless they give you the key to previously unlocked doors, are worse than no leads at all.

Advertising Agencies

Full-service agencies generally have four types of employees: creative people, account managers, media specialists and, sometimes, researchers.

The creatives come up with concepts and work for a creative director. The art director produces design and artwork. Copywriters write the messaging. Account managers coordinate activities between the agency and the client and participate in planning and strategy. Media specialists determine where and when ads should run, based on objectives and budget. Researchers analyze results, study buyer demographics, uncover trends, and quantify market segments.

Traditionally, agencies earn commissions based on the ads their clients place. For example, if the client buys $5,000 worth of ad space in the newspaper, the ad will cost the agency only $4,250 since it receives a 15 percent discount from the media.

Sometimes an agency will charge a fee if the client does not purchase enough advertising space. Others may be willing to work on a performance-based arrangement, which means their compensation is based on business results that can be traced back to their work.

If you choose not to use an outside agency and do your own advertising work, you may be able to set up your own in-house agency and keep the 15 percent. Companies that do this typically use freelancers (contractors) for creative design and copywriting and pay them either a fixed fee or by the hour.

In retail, advertising is an accepted part of the day-to-day costs. Some industrial goods companies, however, shun advertising because of its cost and the difficulties in tracking end results to a specific advertisement. Nonetheless, advertising in business-to-business markets is necessary for two reasons.

The first is there is almost no such thing as a single decision maker in an industrial sale. Instead there are multiple decision makers. Review the upcoming chapter on influencers. Studies show there are more than four buying influences in every industrial purchase and more than two influencers in every consumer purchase. Fewer than half of these people ever talk to a salesperson. Advertising is one way to communicate with these influencers.

Second, advertising lowers your cost of selling. Although advertising is expensive and does have follow-up costs, done correctly it causes prospects to identify themselves to your salespeople—thus shortening the sales cycle.

Before you turn to your agency, though, or begin creating ads yourself, make sure you take the right first steps. Five steps toward creating good advertising are:

- Quantify the business goals. How many products is this campaign supposed to sell or how many leads is it supposed to produce?
- Identify the markets. Where are the prospects?
- Understand the buyers. What kind of people are they? Do they initiate, specify, recommend, or purchase the product?
- Determine the communications objectives. Are you trying to make people aware of you and your product, educate them, change attitudes, or stimulate them into action?
- Create the sales message. What are you going to say to the buyers, in the target markets, to reach the communications objectives, that will result in the desired business results?
- Always include a (CTA) Call to Action that provides the buyer with a simple, easy way to show interest and communicate with the seller. For example, telephone number, web address, and a link to a form.

Whoever creates your advertising must understand your product's positioning, that is, for whom the advertising is intended, what is being offered, and why the customer should be interested. The positioning should be relevant and believable.

Advertise what people find important and what you do best. Include evidence to support your claims. Be careful with testimonials and do not use anonymous quotes. Keep your superlatives to a minimum. Talk directly to the customer. Be specific. "Save $1,000" is much more effective than "Save money." "Save $790" is even better. Pay attention to some of those behavior economics characteristics noted previously.

Print Advertising

Every day, people are bombarded by advertisements on TV, the highways, storefronts, radio, and the Internet. Somehow, your ad must attract attention. Think differently. Think creatively. Think about to whom you're talking. Ask as many people as possible what they think of your ad. When you start to hear the same answers, take them seriously. Run the smallest rendition of the ad first or, if you have only one size, run it in a regional edition or in the lowest-cost publication. Test, test, test.

Pay close attention to every aspect of your ad:

- **Headlines**. Five times more people read headlines than the body copy.
- **Pictures/Visuals**. Headlines and pictures are what people look at first. What you show is often more important than what you say. If the headline and visual don't grab the readers, they will not read the rest of the ad.
- **Captions.** Twice as many people read the caption under the picture as read the body copy.
- **Copy**. Talk directly to the prospect. Use "you" not "your." If it is interesting, the copy can be long. If it isn't interesting, it can't be short enough. Use short sentences and paragraphs. Use subheads. Be enthusiastic.
- **Layout.** Editorial layouts (that look less like ads and more like newspaper articles) are effective. So is the classic ad

layout—visual on top with caption, headline below, followed by the body copy. These two approaches almost always work better than layouts in which the reader must search for the headline and read small, reversed-out type.

- **Multiple impressions.** By the time you are tired of seeing the ad, readers are probably just starting to notice it.
- **Color or black and white?** Only use color if it's needed to show the product to its best advantage. Two-color usually isn't worth the extra money, but four-color works better than black and white. Check the extra charges and then decide.
- **Position (magazine).** The first right-hand page and the back cover are the best. The next best is the second, third, and fourth right-hand pages, in that order. Following are the inside back, front cover, and the page facing the back cover.
- **Bind-In Cards.** These cost about three times the price of a full-page ad and usually get four to eight times the response. They make any position good since the book/ publication tends to open to that page.

Online Advertising

Companies that are switching some of their print ad budgets to online advertising are not just doing this to save money. They are looking for efficiencies and the ability to quickly change and optimize their ads. Web ads are relatively easy to change.

Web advertising shifts the model from intrusion to engagement. A webinar for example, combines the power of direct marketing with the credibility of a personal presentation. It's all about interaction and relationship building. Now you can interact with prospects and immediately provide them with more information. Make your webinar event like. Events draw crowds. Advertise it. Anticipate a fall off between registration and attendance.

The right web campaign will not only bring the right people to the web site, but it will also inform them and answer questions. Done well, online ads make everything happen faster and can be your critical path to shortening sales cycles.

Search Engine Marketing (SEM), one form of web advertising, is particularly effective because it is buyer-seeks-seller oriented in contrast to the seller-seeks-buyer orientation of traditional advertising. Searchers are self-directed, action oriented and easier to target.

When people use a search engine, they are telling you explicitly what they are looking for. This is the kind of critical information that advertisers historically spent lots of time and money trying to gather. Now, search engine marketing analytics programs make it instantly available—a fact we cover later in the book. You simply cannot afford to ignore search engines, especially since two-thirds of Internet users visit them daily.

Online vs Classic Advertising		
Print, TV, Radio Classic Advertising	Your cost is based on the number of impressions, that is, how many people may have glanced at your ad. You hope a decent number remember what you said and call your 800 number.	Seller seeks Buyer. Seller makes the first move.

Online, Digital Advertising Search Engine Marketing, Pay-Per-Click Advertising	Keyword driven. You compete with other advertisers for ad placement by bidding on keywords. Position 1 (top of the page for that keyword or phrase) does not necessarily work best even though it costs the most. Top of page, 1 thru 3 or 4, all provide the most exposure and likelihood of engagement.	Buyer seeks Seller. Buyer makes the first move. You, the advertiser, only pay when someone shows interest and clicks on your ad

As you would surmise from the above, it is no wonder that digital advertising, where you only pay when someone shows interest, has become the advertising medium of choice all over the world.

Getting the Message Right

Before you tell everyone your product looks better, tastes best, or goes the fastest, be prepared to prove it will perform as advertised. Consider your prospect's emotional side. Appealing to reason makes sense but adding an emotional appeal can transform a left-brained, logical sales message into one that's far more effective and memorable.

Co-Op Advertising Pros and Cons

Co-ops occur when two parties, such as a manufacturer and retailer/reseller, share the costs of a marketing communication program such as a mailing or advertising campaign. Some co-ops are done very well, like the American Express' co-ops with restaurants.

But be careful. Your piece of the message can easily get lost. Control, clutter, and timing problems can result in a campaign indistinguishable from others. Mixed messages lose focus and impact, and there is always a good chance that your co-op partner will not have the same motives you have.

There are, however, at least two occasions when co-ops make a lot of sense. One is when you have a new product for a new market that is populated with potential customers who know nothing about you or your product. A co-op venture with another firm that is already credible in your new market can do wonders to help you get your unknown firm and product off the ground.

Co-op ads also make sense when the media costs are out of your league and the co-op partner is putting up half or more. Under those conditions, and assuming the audience is right, I'd figure out some way to get the money.

Wrap Up

- What's your message?
- What keywords or keyword phrases work best?
- With a pencil and paper, outline a classic ad: headline, visual, caption, body copy, call to action.

Chapter 16: Direct Response Marketing

Think of this as a (CTA) Call to action. It's the difference between saying to someone, "I could use your help moving this box" and "Help me move this box."

Most companies need some mix of direct response and awareness advertising. If you have a limited advertising budget, direct response is usually a better choice since it is more proactive, easier to track, and likely to produce faster results.

No marketing program will succeed without your sales representatives' enthusiastic support. So, before you embark on a direct marketing program, talk to your own sales representatives. They know what's going on in their territories, their local competition, and the spheres of influence

They need to know beforehand what the marketing program is all about and when it's going to happen. They are a critical component of the project, since they will follow up the best leads and secure the sale. When the program has concluded, ask them if they think it was worth the effort. They'll know better than anybody.

Direct Response Advertising

What you are trying to do is to stimulate prospects into action rather than simply to remind them you are in business. Direct response ads have several parts:

- A definite offer to the prospect. The offer might be a free report, or it might be an actual product or service. If the ad asks for an order, you must include the price, and the terms and conditions of sale.
- All the information necessary to decide. Therefore, many direct response ads are lengthy. If you are trying to get the reader to buy right from the ad, you'll need to take your customer through each phase of the sales cycle. That means attention-getting headlines and subheads, relevant benefits, evidence that you can deliver as promised, an offer, and a way for the reader to say yes.
- A response device, like a telephone number or order coupon. This is the close—the asking for the order part. Make certain it is clear and unambiguous.
- Lead handling. Consider this. Studies show that at any time, only about 3 percent of your market's prospective buyers are ready to make a purchase now. If your campaign focuses on trying to close that 3 percent, you'll be ignoring the 5-7 percent who are open to buy, but not today and the 25-30 percent who are interested and just need more information. That's why direct response pros do not write "selling" ads, instead they write "lead generating" ads, for example, a call to action like "Free White Paper on how to..." This way instead of going after 3 percent, you'll be going after 40 percent.

Differences Between Direct Response and General Advertising	
Direct Response Advertising	General Advertising
Directed to individuals in a market segment that are identifiable by name, address, and purchase behavior. Narrower targeting increases the open rates (percentage of subscribers who open the email).	Mass selling to broad groups with common demographics.

The medium is the marketplace.	The retail outlet is the marketplace.
Marketer controls product delivery.	Marketer may lose control once product enters a distribution channel.
Used to motivate an immediate order or inquiry.	Used for cumulative effect over time to build awareness.
Repetition used within ad.	Repetition used over time.
Consumers feel high perceived risk. Products are bought unseen. Recourse is distant.	Consumers feel less risk. Products can be seen. Have direct recourse.

Buying Motives

Wants and needs are very much affected by times, trends, and fads. What's in one year is out the next. When determining your sales message, stay tuned in to exactly who you are talking to, where they are coming from, and what's likely to be on their minds.

What's in it for me? Greed is a great motivator. Instant gratification is almost as good. And both are on the rise. Society and advertisers take advantage of these human qualities. That's why lotteries make billions and credit card debt is ever increasing—especially among those who can't afford the purchase.

Understanding your customer's psychographics is just as important as having a great product. In many cases, customers will opt for lesser products if they think they're getting a deal, or they can get it now or it will impress others.

In the spirit of selling feelings, not things, the first two Wants and Needs below, Fit In and Gain Status, seem to be the be the most common emotional reasons why people buy,

Customer Wants and Needs	
Fit In	Gain status
Make money	Better health
Save time and effort	Impress others

Win praise	Save money
Security	Be in style
Attract opposite sex	Popularity
Have fun	Self-improvement
Help others	Competitive edge
Get a bargain	Better performance

Awareness and Brand Advertising

Reminding people you merely exist is generally a great waste of money. So does promoting your brand and not the products. People don't buy brands; they buy the real tangible things that deliver both the practical and emotional results they crave. They buy products that solve their problems and make them feel good. And their buying motives are driven by how the product is framed/advertised/described.

Email Marketing

Email is an effective direct response advertising medium. It's accountable, has low production costs, is easily changed, and has no postage or printing expenses. Email is not just about pushing a product or selling something. It can be used to engage people, increase their brand awareness, and give them a better understanding of what you're all about. It's also a quick and cost-effective way to test messaging and offers.

Your recipient's mailbox is very likely overflowing, so before you do a major roll out, do some list hygiene. Also do some testing. Test the subject line, the offer, the frequency, and different list segments. Mobile users are almost certainly part of your market, so make sure the email displays properly on a cell phone. And personalize your email. When a person sees your email addressed to him/her, it suggests you have at least some level of awareness you are addressing a distinct human being.

Couponing

Marketers use coupons to sell excess inventory, find new uses for an old product, introduce new products, and stimulate overall demand. Because of its effectiveness, couponing has become a powerful tool for many businesses.

Customers use coupons to save money, try new items, buy impulse items (one in four coupons is used for products buyers don't need immediately), and because it makes them feel smart.

Nowhere is couponing more effective than in the package goods industry. Data shows coupon clippers account for 43 percent of disposable diaper sales, 35 percent of ready-to-eat cereal sales, and 29 percent of liquid detergent sales.

Coupons are typically distributed through co-ops; that is, by manufacturers in conjunction with one another. The most popular vehicle is still the Sunday newspaper, which accounts for nearly 80 percent of all coupons distributed in the United States. Other distribution techniques include package inserts, in-store dispensers, cash register receipts, newspaper inserts, co-op mailings, special interest groups and, of course, the Internet—where digital coupons have become increasingly popular.

Internet savvy consumers find coupons on Facebook and on coupon aggregation web sites such as RetailMeNot, CouponChief.com and Savings.com. Coupons are even available on your cell phone via services like Verve Wireless and Cellfire.

Direct Mail

Do the open-the-mail-over-the-garbage-can test. The direct mail you don't throw in immediately got your attention.

Direct mail is a private medium. Postage rate increases notwithstanding, direct mail is still viable. However, mailing to a large group can be cost prohibitive. Personalized digital printing enables you to print fewer pieces cost effectively.

We noted previously that email should be personalized; the same goes for direct mail. If the next chapter were on selling over the phone, or selling in person, personalization would also be front and center. The most effective marketing and selling programs are almost always personal. Or at least they appear to be. Yet, less than 50 percent of the nearly 200 billion pieces of mail the post office receives annually is personalized.

Response rates

Unless you are mailing to people you have mailed to before, it is impossible to approximate what percentage will respond to your mailing. Assume your response rate will be less than 1 percent. According to surveys, in general, only 6 to 7 percent of an audience that never heard of you, will pay attention to your message. The other 90 percent aren't ready or don't care. I'm not sure I believe all that, but I can tell you that 1) when mailing to strangers, you can't expect much more than a 1 percent response and 2) you need to be able to make money on response rates of greater than 1 percent.

Markups or gross margins

To make a profit, you'll need to sell enough to more than cover the cost of the mailing and overhead. Therefore, you'll need markups of at least three to five times your cost of goods. Most companies selling through direct mail have at least that.

Mail costs

How much can you afford to spend on the mail piece? The actual cost of the piece (creative, printing, materials, paper) must be added to the cost of the mailing list, postage costs, and whatever labor it takes to get it into the mailbox. To show a profit, mail costs should not exceed more than 50 percent of the sales they produce. That's why you need those markups.

Sales costs

These are the variable costs you incur every time someone responds. They include the cost of the 800 number telephone calls, telemarketer, and credit card processing costs.

Selling

As in any selling situation, three primary factors are involved:

1. *To whom you are selling (mailing)*

2. What you are selling, and

3. How you present your wares.

Some direct mailers refer to the 50-40-10 rule. 50 percent of the effectiveness of your direct mail program depends on your list—to whom you are mailing. Another 40 percent depends on what you are selling and your ad copy; only 10 percent of the program's effectiveness depends on the layout. In other words, having the right product for the right person at the right time is more important than a dazzling presentation.

The best creative strategies tend to have a single, clear objective—an issue relevant to the person and the business. Use easy-to-understand language and short sentences. Evoke passion, radiate energy, and make it interesting. Try bribery. Give them a free this and that. Just make sure your cost of goods still meets your business model. Make it hard for the prospect to say no.

Finally, establish your response goals. Determine beforehand the ratio of orders-to-inquiries you need to make the program successful. And don't get discouraged. Research shows that 40 percent of the people who have responded to direct mail in the past will do it again and buy from someone in the next twelve months.

Income Statement for Direct Mail Campaign, 5,000 Pieces Mailed. Number of Orders = 100. Response Rate = 2% Average Order Value = $42.50			
Revenue:			
Products @ $38.00 ea.	$3,800.00		Customer pays $38.00
Shipping & handling	$450.00		Plus $4.50 shipping ea.
Total Revenue	$4,250.00	100%	
Cost of Goods:			
Product cost.	$950.00		Each cost $9.50
Shipping & handling costs	$400.00		Plus $4.00 each
Total Cost of Goods	$1,350.00	32%	
Operating Expenses:			
Variable Sales Costs: 800#, Credit Card Handling	$212.50	5%	$2.12 per order
Mail Costs:			
Envelope, letter, $.10 ea.	$500.00		
Postage $.19 ea.	$950.00		
Name $.08 ea.	$400.00		
Labor $.03 ea.	$150.00		
Total Mail Costs:	$2,000.00	47%	
Overhead	$340.00	8%	
Pre-tax profit	$340.00	8%	

Direct mail testing

Mailing to new prospects, or people you don't know, is risky and expensive; mailing to total strangers is rarely profitable. Direct mail profits are usually directly proportional to the ratio of old customer names to new prospect names. So, testing new prospect lists is vitally important.

Testing is not quite as simple as renting a few thousand names from various lists and then rolling out to the lists that tested best.

That's because some list brokers may rent you only the list's best names for the test. This, of course, leaves lower quality names for the roll out.

Here is how to avoid this: Don't leave it up to the broker. Choose the test names yourself. For example, order all the names in a set of zip codes.

When you test your advertisement, use two renditions that have only one difference (for example, a different headline) between them. Make the one that works best your control piece. The next time you test, change something else.

B2B Direct Mail

In business-to-business, direct mail is often used to generate leads instead of orders. The idea is to uncover qualified prospects—to stimulate potential buyers to identify themselves. For products or services requiring a live sales call, the objective is to get the prospect to agree to meet with a salesperson. In this situation, it is usually a good idea to use a telemarketer to further qualify first-level responses. Save your expensive salespeople for face-to-face selling with qualified prospects.

Since the objective of most business-to-business mailings is leads and not immediate orders, it is more difficult to measure success directly. Contrast this to consumer mailings, the success of which can be measured by the number of orders you take over the phone or the Internet.

Business-to-business mail campaigns also tend to be relatively expensive since there are usually a series of mailings, or other follow-ups, versus a single mailing to a consumer.

It is also more difficult to get the right contact names for business-to-business mailings. That's because:

- More than one person in a company will be involved in deciding,

- Names are harder to acquire (many business names are merely titles, and people often change jobs and responsibilities), and
- Direct mail gets screened by mail rooms/secretaries who are liable to discard mail they consider unimportant.

Another difference between consumer and business-to-business prospects is that business prospects are not making decisions that will affect them personally. That is, the decision will not benefit them directly. Consumers, of course, buy for themselves. Many business prospects do buy for personal reasons, but these are usually difficult to predetermine, and better left to your salesperson to uncover.

In business-to-business mailings, 75 percent or higher waste is common. For every 100 pieces mailed, only 25 ever get into the hands of the addressee. Fewer are read. Several problems contribute to this. For example, one firm may operate under several different names at the same address. Then there are all those one-person firms that operate out of garages. Duplications can be difficult to find because many people use the same address. And the person who opens the mail is usually not the person you are trying to reach. This, incidentally, is one of the reasons why putting your sales letters and literature in with packages and invoices is not a good idea in business mailings.

With direct mail you control when and how many people you mail. All business responses need to be followed up immediately; so only mail as many as you can handle on the back end. Each day a lead is not acted upon lowers the likelihood of conversion. Telemarketing follow-ups should be quick and personal. Have your telemarketer (or salesperson) follow-up every lead with questions such as

- Are you and your firm interested in our products?
- Which one?
- Why?

- Pricing ranges from x to y.
- Are you planning on purchasing within the next ____ days?
- Would you like to have a salesperson call on you?
- Let me make sure I have your correct name and address.
- Are there others in your firm who should know more about our products?

Measure, document, and track your results. This enables you to measure against the original objectives as well as prove value to the sales force and to management.

Here is one approach to writing a direct mail letter:

- Think about the best sales pitches you ever made. Try and recreate what went on in each situation. Then, record each of your best sales pitches. If you have salespeople working for you, record their best sales pitches as well.
- Transcribe each presentation. Get a pair of scissors—literally or figuratively—and cut out every paragraph of each pitch. Sort the paragraphs into three piles: features and facts about the product, benefits of buying the product, and war stories and background information.
- Take the pile with the stories and put them aside for a different approach. For this one, prioritize the features and put the paragraphs in priority order. Do the same with the benefits. You are now ready to write a sales letter.

Features and Benefits Sales Letter

Dear Sam,

I heard you were in the market for a new van. I have a great one and I'm getting ready to sell it. You should be interested because the van has several outstanding features. It has:

Dual air bags, steel body, heavy-duty shocks, and an over-size gas tank.

Four-wheel drive along with a 275 horsepower, six-cylinder engine.

A 300-watt stereo radio with eight speakers, sub-woofer, iPod connectivity, and a CD player.

And a lot more great features.

These features have made this the most popular van in the market today. Here are more benefits of owning a van like mine:

It's safe, rugged, and always brings you back.

It's powerful enough to get you anywhere quickly, regardless of the terrain.

It's literally a concert hall on wheels. You've never heard sound like this.

You'll be amazed at how many people will admire and complement you for owing such a great vehicle.

I doubt my van will be on the market very long because I am offering it at a very attractive price. If you're interested, call me immediately at 123-4567.

Sincerely,

Wrap Up

Aside from the purchase of very basic necessities, people buy for personal reasons such as to fit in or for status or to achieve superior health. Buyers are more motivated by how the product is framed/marketed than by the actual item.

The three most important parts of a direct mail campaign: list, list, list.

Chapter 17: Telemarketing

Telemarketing is quick, personal, and almost mandatory when someone has responded to a mailer or advertisement or has downloaded something from your web site. In business-to-business mailings, prospects expect a follow-up call.

Don't try to accomplish too much over the phone. Use the call to qualify, set appointments, and gather market data. In other words, an essential ingredient in the call is *listening.* If it's a cold call, as with direct mail, start with a good prospect list. Then develop a computerized database for future correspondence, mailings, and announcements.

Provide your telemarketers with scripts that tell them exactly what to say to everyone they may encounter—the receptionist, the protective administrative assistant, the prospect. Include scripted answers to the most frequently asked questions. Make sure they confirm the spelling of the prospect's name, title, and department. Have them ask uninterested or unqualified prospects if there is anyone else in that company that would be interested in what you are selling.

Some people worry that a telemarketer's lack of product knowledge will turn off a prospective buyer. Certainly, that's possible, but for anything other than calling the busiest and most important people, it's more efficient to use a telemarketer—even when you're selling something requiring lots of product knowledge.

It really doesn't take a lot of training or skill to recognize Mr. or Ms. Right for your product. A prospect will usually let you know quickly if he or she has any interest at all. Therefore, listening is at least as important as informing when it comes to telemarketing.

Let me share with you a personal example of just how effective telemarketing can be. I could call this one of the smartest things I ever did as a salesman.

Years ago, I was a salesman in Los Angeles selling capital equipment to aerospace firms. At that stage in my career I was worried about only one thing—making quota and keeping my job.

In those days, I did my own prospecting and regularly ignored the leads provided to me by the home office. I ignored them because the leads were unqualified and simply not worth the time it would take to find the few qualified prospects from the bunch. Nonetheless, I always had some guilt feelings about not even bothering to phone any of the forty or so names that would arrive each month.

One day, I heard a new admin talking to a customer on the phone and she was charming. I complimented her and she told me she "just loved to call people up and talk to them."

To make a long story short, I wrote her a script and had her start calling the leads I never bothered calling. Her job was to find someone who answered yes to four questions:

Are you in the market for our type of product?

Do you have the authority to buy and can you and your company afford at least $30,000?

Will you be buying in the next 90 days?

Would you like our salesman to come visit you?

When she got a yes to all four questions, I would slip her a little cash. After a while, my new account business picked up dramatically. It got so good I had to change the last question to "Will you come visit us at our office, meet with Mr. Hughes, and see a demonstration?" Now that really worked!

Imagine. I would walk into the office and there would be a qualified buyer (a person I had never met or talked to) waiting to see me about buying my product. I would first invite him/her into my office and take about 5 or 10 minutes to re-qualify. Then, I would call in our demonstration person who would spend the next 30 to 45 minutes showing the prospect how the products worked. At first, I would go with them, but I soon discovered it wasn't necessary. Instead, I would close my office door, put my feet up on the desk, and read the *LA Times* sports section.

A half an hour later, there would be a knock on my door, and I would pick it up from there. Overnight, I became the top new account salesperson in the company—without doing the hard work and without having to travel the freeways of Los Angeles. Remember: I was the same guy who was just making quota.

Looking back, I suppose there were more cost-effective ways for management to have handled my problem than allowing me to commandeer an employee to become my personal prospecting assistant. I probably should have done some of that prospecting myself, and I certainly shouldn't have been reading the sport pages (I was young, cocky, and not the mature adult I now claim to be). However, I can say, without question, that using a trained telemarketer to follow up on all my inquiries was really one of the smartest things I ever did as a salesman.

Wrap Up

This is a hustle business. Just do it. He/she who makes the most calls wins.

Chapter 18: Media Releases

News sells.

Some people call a press release, or media release, free advertising. A press release is never free. It takes time, skill, and money to write articles and releases, and interact with the media. Access to decent databases of media contacts also costs money. The free online release distribution services are generally worth what you pay for them.

Media Release vs Advertising	
Media Release	Advertising
Hope for it to run	Pay for it to run
News	Product information
Out of your control (you typically don't know when a story it triggers will run)	Under your control (you determine when it will run)
Credible (usually)	Biased

There are many reasons why press releases are popular. For one thing, they are easy to create and publish, especially on the Internet. They also make great ride-alongs in your mailings; stick one in the envelope or attach it to the email. For another, a press release potentially helps you reach the large percentage of people who won't see or read your ads. Further, there is always an implied third-party endorsement from the medium. Finally, rising media costs make any alternative to buying advertising space worth considering.

When a public company sends a press announcement out on the newswires, the search engines automatically and immediately display the release's headlines and sub-headlines. No more waiting for someone to decide if your news is worth publishing. And, whether you're a public company or not, you will certainly want to display your press announcements on your own web site and on any social sites in which you participate.

An effective press release strategy considers more than the consumer or buyer. It also considers industry influencers. The idea is to communicate with the 10 percent of your market that influences the other 90 percent. You want to reach people like market/application experts, editors, major account users, commentators, and even competitors. And don't forget the financial types; they are always looking for evidence to justify their existing or potential investments or recommendations.

Newsworthy items worth submitting to the media include:

- New product introductions or enhancements
- Financial results
- New executives and promotions
- Innovative business approaches
- Trade show participation
- Contract wins, new client sign-ups
- Mergers, acquisitions, joint ventures
- Awards, speeches, seminars
- Availability of research papers

News releases are only one approach to interacting with the media. Feature articles, TV, and radio/podcast appearances, and speaking engagements can be even more effective, and a good media release can lead to all of them.

Feature articles are normally coordinated with and pre-authorized by an editor. To initiate an article, follow the submission guidelines posted on the media outlet's website. A typical process is sending a letter to the editor outlining your idea and promising exclusivity to the publication. If the article runs, get reprints.

Make sure you put TV, radio stations, and podcasts on your media list since they are constantly looking for talk show guests. Just because you have interesting news does not mean you are a candidate for a slot on a radio or TV show, however. Producers must be very picky about only putting people on the air who can help the host hold audience interest. If you want to do radio, podcasts, and TV, be sure that you have footage available on YouTube, Vimeo, and/or your website so a producer can see you in action.

Speaking engagements are also great ways to leverage your best presentation. After you've already gotten yourself booked for a few presentations, and had at least one of them videotaped, then you can contact speakers' bureaus. But be prepared for rejection by the bureaus unless you already have done paid speaking engagements and can provide clips through the venues mentioned above. Speakers' bureaus can find you an engagement and audience. Be prepared to pay them a fee.

Create a press kit that includes a background piece on your company, brief biographies on your key personnel, and at least one newsworthy announcement. The kit should be available in print and downloadable from your website.

The most efficient way to create a list of current, relevant media contacts is get access to one of the public relations databases available to PR professionals. The service will guide you in creating a customized list that includes both email and mailing addresses; make sure you include contacts from trade and professional associations on your list.

Keep your message short. According to the PR pros, “When you practice your story, stand on one foot. If the other comes down before you’re finished, your pitch is too long.”

Establish a style guide for all your company communications. Establish precise rules for punctuation, when to use abbreviation, and capitalization. For example, if you capitalize a product name, then it must always be capitalized. This goes for your company positioning; it should always appear exactly the way it was originally written.

Here are ten press release tips:

1. Include one idea per release and put it in the headline. State the news angle clearly and concisely in the first one or two sentences.
2. Include quotes from the one or two principal spokespeople related to the story.
3. Make them easy to read by double spacing and restricting word count to no more than 400 words, if possible.
4. Include a photo if relevant.
5. When you contact an editor, by email or phone, keep the pitch brief and to the point—and address the person by name. “Dear Editor,” is rude.
6. If an editor starts to ask for your opinion, give it. Build a relationship.
7. Press releases should answer the key interrogatives—who, what, when, where, and why—as soon as possible.
8. Never discuss advertising with an editor. Interest in your story is not a matter of quid pro quo.
9. If an editor makes a mistake, use discretion. Unless it is a major problem, do nothing.
10. If an editor does a good job, send a complimentary note.

Press Release Ingredients

Newsworthy, relevant, and accurate information makes a press release worth reading. Let's assume you're writing about a new contract announcement. To begin with, you will want to name the customer exactly the way they name themselves. For example, use "The Kroger Co.," not "Kroger Stores." Make sure the spelling is perfect. If the customer doesn't want their name in print, then use something like "a major US retailer." Then tell the readers what they would want to know:

- What did they buy from you?
- What will the product do for the buyer, that is, why did they need the product?
- Is there something interesting about what the product does? If so, mention it and if it's interesting enough, use it in the subhead.
- Why did they buy from you and not from someone else?
- How much money did they spend?
- Is this contract a one-time event? Or the first of many?
- When will you deliver the goods?
- How does this order fit with your company's overall business plan?
- How could someone else order the same kind of thing from you?

Press Release Format

Use descriptive headlines and sub-headlines. Many readers won't read any further, so try and tell the whole story right there. Use keywords so the search engines can deliver your release to the right people.

Note: According to *Adweek*, journalists read as many as fifty press releases every week and spend less than one-minute on each.

When asked their preferred style of release they said they would like the information in bullet form, which allows them to easily add their own content like links to websites, and so on.

Headline: ABC wins $1,000,000 contract from the Baron Hotel chain for (use keywords here) services.

Sub-headline: (Keywords) from ABC will be featured by Hotel Chain in national TV advertising. Contract includes options for annual renewals and additional services.

Try to get an endorsement quote from the customer. Use a quote from someone in your company on how the order is in line with the company's master plan. Include links to videos, and other supplemental sources of information to make the release interactive

If your company is public, slant the release toward investors. Use investor keywords here. End it with a safe harbor statement (warns the reader that the press release contains "forward-looking statements" that may or may not come true).

Use an "About Our Company" subhead followed by a paragraph—like your positioning statement—that describes your company. The last sentence of the paragraph should have your telephone number and web address. Again, sprinkle keywords throughout. If appropriate, do the same thing for the other company, that is, a subhead followed by a paragraph about them that includes their contact information. Below is a sample paragraph for ABC.

About ABC: Founded in 2010, ABC specializes in providing custom-designed visitor monitoring services and equipment for hotels with 200 or fewer rooms for rent. ABC products and services enable smaller hotels to provide four-star visitor safety services to their guests at affordable prices and without having to hire any additional personnel. Clients include xxx, xxx, and xxx. Corporate headquarters is in Buffalo, NY. Call xxx-xxx-xxxx or visit www.xxxxxx.com for more information.

Wrap Up

Whether it's print or online: get your news up front in the headline, in the sub-headline, and in the first sentences of the release.

Chapter 19: Broadcast Media

Television, radio, and podcasts draw devoted audiences daily. For generations, radio and TV have been powerful advertising venues, but with the advent of streaming, podcasts have joined them in becoming important ways to reach customers.

Radio and podcast audiences are measured in number of listeners. TV audiences are measured in number of households.

Reach is the term used to measure the number of different homes or listeners exposed to a message within a given time segment. Frequency measures how many times the average listener/viewer will hear/see the message over a given time segment.

Radio and Podcasts Feel Personal

Reasons for radio's popularity—and we can now add podcasts to that as well—include its relatively low cost, personal nature, and its niche market appeal. The cost to advertise on radio is very low compared to television. Podcast sponsorship is typically a cost/listens (for example, $20 per 1000 listens for a 15-second spot) or cost/purchase, meaning that your cost depends on how many listeners become buyers.

People listen to radio and podcasts in their cars, while jogging, in the bathroom, cooking dinner. It can have a powerful emotional appeal. Research indicates that people remember what they hear more readily and vividly than they remember what they see.

Thus, radio and podcasts are very flexible and useful for target marketing. With these broadcast media you can carve up a market into far more specific segments than you can with mass-reach media.

Radio rating sheets tell you the demographics of a station's audience. Station formats and programming schedules also reveal the psychographics (lifestyle characteristics, preferences) of that audience. Podcasts have similar data, often with even more finely tuned information on market segmentation than radio shows tend to have. For example, car aficionados would not just have a single car show, like NPR's classic show *Car Talk*; they could be listening to a podcast about British classic cars, American hot rods, or DeLoreans.

Drive times have the largest audiences and are most expensive. But these are not necessarily the best times for direct response since the driver is unlikely to be able to write down your telephone number, let alone call. Radio listeners tend to tune-in regularly to the same station, with little switching, so you may have to buy time on several stations to meet your reach goals.

With podcasts, you don't have the same concern. Even though your target customer may listen in drive time, the show could always be replayed at will.

Effective radio advertising identifies your product and benefits quickly and repeats them often. A straight monologue is the equivalent of talking heads on TV. Dialogue between two people, humor, and music can make your radio advertising more effective. Multiple impressions work as well in this medium as they do in print campaigns. Thus, you are better off bunching your radio ads rather than running the same number of ads over longer time periods.

Television Is Still the Big Time

Television is an action medium and a perfect place to demonstrate your product. Instead of telling them, show them. Just like in print advertising, you have precious few seconds to grab the viewer's attention, so a visually appealing, provocative lead is desirable.

TV can be very effective per dollar spent; however, production and time costs are very high. TV is perceived by viewers as being an expensive place to advertise. Thus, your company's prestige and credibility are enhanced when viewers see you can afford this.

Take advantage of the medium. Use demonstrations, close-ups, sound effects, and animation. Your advertising concept must, in just a few seconds, jolt a lethargic and jaded audience to attention.

People often remember the commercial but forget the name of the product. Mention the product name early and often. If you have budget problems, TV may not be the right place for you. You can, however, save money by eliminating actors, not going on location, minimizing animation, avoiding original music, and forgetting about expensive celebrities.

Cable television has traditionally been a lower cost alternative to broadcast television; however, the popularity of some cable shows has thrown them into a different category. With cable, the audience is more highly defined. In fact, cable and streaming services have many of the same traits of radio and special interest magazines; the companies that collect the audiences' money every month have a good sense of what they are watching.

With a much smaller, but more targeted audience, cable is a great approach for vertical market products or merchants serving local, geographic markets. Not only are the time costs much lower, but the production costs can be as well, since viewers on these channels don't expect expensive, high-production-value commercials. You may also save money by using Google TV Ads, which lets you bid for cable TV time.

Programmatic TV

Traditional TV advertising is bought and sold the old fashion way, without reliance on real-time digital data. Programmatic TV is TV ad buying that uses real-time or near real-time data and automation to target consumer segments and the right end-users with precision. Programmatic TV ad spending in the US is projected to be $4.73 billion in 2020 vs $2.77 billion in 2019, a 70.9 percent increase. (https://emarketer.com/content/programmatic-tv-automation-is-improving-but-pain-points-still-exist)

Shopping Channels

Retailing today, like everything else, is being driven by efficiency and information. Consumers want more information because they want to save time. Shopping channels are natural alternatives for people who want to shop more efficiently yet still feel as though they are encountering a "salesclerk." Anyone who has purchased something from a TV shopping channel probably knows that the customer service people hired to interface with the customer tend to project a personal interest in the buyer: "Hi, my name is Sharon and I'm happy to answer your questions..." Interactive, multimedia television shopping has become more commonplace and is a real and natural alternative to retail outlets.

Infomercials are a billion-dollar industry, and the reason is that they work. Infomercials are the longer than two-minute (long form), DRTV (Direct Response Television) commercials that give buyers all the information they need to order the product right now—over the phone or Internet. DRTV campaigns are usually managed by specialist agencies that help with the creative content and the media buys, which often include remnant time on cable. The most effective infomercials use celebrity announcers and are filled with demonstrations and satisfied customers. They sell products with broad appeal; think of all the infomercials you've seen for products that make you thinner, healthier, prettier, happier, or cleaner.

The financial picture for DRTV is like that of direct mail, that is, you'll need large markups on the products being sold (at least 4 times cost) to have any chance of making a profit. For example, if you sold $2,000 worth of products that cost you $400 (a 5x markup), your gross profit would be $1,600. If it cost you $1,000 of DRTV time to realize that $2,000 in sales, then you would have $600 left over to pay for other expenses, yourself, and profit.

Wrap Up

Local television is still effective and affordable. Not only does it attract buyers, it's also great for publicity. Suddenly, strangers will recognize you and tell you they saw you on TV.

Chapter 20: Trade Shows

Fifty face-to-face sales calls in a day—that's how I see trade shows.

Trade shows are a great way to talk to many prospects in a short period of time. The bulk of this chapter is about exhibiting at a trade show. First, however let me tell you how I recently learned a valuable lesson: how to work a trade show as an attendee.

My client was exhibiting at a small trade show in Baltimore, Maryland. There were less than a hundred vendors, most in ten-foot-wide booths across six or so aisles. Ours was in the last aisle.

I arrived at the show, walked it, and ultimately took a seat in the rear of our booth. Our sales guys were up front. I looked out and noticed a young woman visiting one of the booths further up the aisle. I then noticed she visited the next one and was working her way to ours. I was curious, so I paid attention.

This nicely dressed, woman arrived at our booth, got the attention of one of salesmen, and said something like, "My name is xxx, my company is yyy, we make the finest zzz in the entire nation. If your company has any interest or need for zzz, please have the appropriate person give me a call. Nobody does zzz better than yyy." While she was giving her 20-second pitch, she was removing her high-quality business card from an expensive looking holder.

I instantly liked what l saw. I motioned to her and asked her how well her approach was working. She said, this was the first time she had ever tried it at a trade show. And, that she had started on the first aisle a few hours earlier. By the time she got to the end of that aisle, she had pretty much got it down to what she did with us. She said several people in the booths had given her the name of the person she should be contacting and, in a few cases, that person was in the booth and she had made appointments to visit them. I was impressed.

Two weeks later, the scene shifted to Washington DC where one of the big information technology firms was announcing a new something at a local hotel. It was a professional presentation, demonstration and sales pitch accompanied by free hors d'oeuvres and drinks. To get into the room with the free food and drinks, you had to enter through an adjoining room, where there were six other companies with table-top displays working the attendees as they filed in for the freebies. Just as I was about to do just that, ignore the sellers and get a good seat near the refreshments, I thought of that young lady in Baltimore. I just had to do what she had done. So, I did just that at each of the six vendor's tables. One of them ended up being one of our biggest new customers that year.

Exhibiting

Exhibiting at a trade show is hard work but it can be fun. It is also an opportunity to put your team on stage, mix it up with the competition, and make lots of contacts.

Don't just staff your booth with salespeople. Take the people who know the product best, for example, the product managers or the designers. Take the president. Just make sure you have at least one sales/marketing type and one person who can always answer detailed questions on duty.

Trade shows can be very effective. In just a few days, you can:

- Make sales
- Uncover new prospects

- Introduce new products
- Increase market awareness
- Solidify manufacturer/reseller relationships
- Test market new products or marketing ideas
- Check out the competition
- Meet the press and industry influencers

Choose a booth that doesn't cost a fortune to ship or assemble. It should also be modular so that it works in multiples of ten-foot spaces. Pick a spot near a company that will have a large draw. Use the aisles—if you are demonstrating, have your attendees spill over into the aisles.

Have all the people working your booth memorize a two-to-four sentence statement of what your firm does and why the prospect should be interested (the benefit). Dress comfortably. No eating or drinking in the booth. Answer the exact question posed by the prospect. Talk to only one person at a time. Make sure your president talks to customers and prospects. Go to the parties.

Don't put on elaborate presentations; the attention span just isn't there. Rather than hand out expensive brochures to people already overburdened with literature, take their names, and mail or email them something. Try not to spend more than five minutes with any one prospect. Use giveaways, make sure they have your contact info on them

Most trade shows provide visitors with encoded name badges that can be swiped and read into a centralized database. If this is not available, you'll need some centralized place to store all the leads. You do not want salespeople putting leads into their pockets.

A typical follow-up to a trade show includes a mailing from headquarters with a follow-up telephone call a week or so after the mailing.

Trade Show Pros and Cons	
Pros	Cons
Make hundreds of contacts in a few days	Information overload for attendees
Instant feedback	Can be expensive
Contacting the press and industry influencers is good for credibility	Too much time spent with people who aren't buyers
Gather competitive data, uncover new opportunities	Requires salespeople to spend too much time away from their territories

Presenting at a trade show or putting on a special event is always expensive, that is, there are travel, lodging and other costs involved.

To gage effectiveness of the show or event, create a mechanism for gathering statistics. Use email to ask attendees before the event what they will be looking for and ask them afterwards if they were satisfied.

To boost attendance, use email to advertise. Give incentives for early sign-ups. Ask your presenters to notify their friends and contacts; use social networks to spread the word.

Webcasts

Instead of traveling to a trade show/event to deliver a presentation, try webcasting. Advertise the live event and take questions using any of the many webcast services. Archive the webcast and make it available on your website for future viewing at the visitor's convenience.

Live webinars are excellent ways to communicate your message and they are great attention getters; an upcoming webinar is newsworthy information you can use to promote your upcoming webinar via a press announcement, your website, email, blog, social media, and telephone. You can also source websites such as brighttalk.com and on24.com to help you create a first-class, professional presentation and leverage their internal webinar promotional tools.

Wrap Up

Exhibiting and attending a trade show can be a day well spent. It's where the buyers are. You'll be exposed to multiple prospective buyers, influencers, vendors, and more.

Remember how that woman in Baltimore worked the crowd. Create your own 20-second spiel.

Chapter 21: Sales Collateral

Digital sales collateral such as case studies, press announcements, and white papers are very effective, cost nothing and are easy to find and deliver. Online and print sales presentations should help move prospects through each step in the sales cycle. Plan both your online and print sales presentations accordingly. If the presentation you're going to create is intended for total strangers, concentrate on benefits. If it's intended for prospects nearing a decision, concentrate on facts and figures.

As you would when planning a presentation, consider the five classic selling steps when designing sales literature:

1. **Attention.** You have one chance to make a first impression. At a minimum, you will need a business card and stationery. You may also need an email introduction, or sales letters for prospecting purposes.
2. **Interest.** Now that prospects know who you are and what you do, they'll need more details to start believing you. This is where an online video, webinar, or seminar can work.
3. **Conviction.** To turn a prospect into a customer, you may need evidence—hard facts that say you and your product will deliver as promised. Get your print collateral, data sheets, testimonials, letters of recommendation online and accessible.

4. **Desire.** By now, your prospects should be convinced that they can use what you sell. Now you need to make them want it. Use success stories, and before/after comparisons.
5. **Close.** You need price lists and contracts.

Think of your business cards as mini brochures. Quality and look are important. Consider a card with rounded edges or slightly large shape. Use extra copy to define what you do. Fold-over cards provide extra space to properly position your business and allow you to be more precise about what you deliver.

Make sure all your print collateral is available on your website and social networks. Ad reprints should be low cost and inexpensive to mail. A brochure can be anything from a text-only description of what you do on your own stationary, to a four-color piece with pictures and graphics. Use an outside graphics art firm if you are doing anything elaborate.

Even if you are distributing through electronic means only, design is critical. Design elements that include well-placed hyper-links, for example, are key to driving your prospect's attention to a decision-making place.

If you insist on doing it yourself, use one of the pre-formatted layouts that are typically available with the latest word processing and publishing packages. Designers have participated in creating the templates and they reflect good, basic sense of how to appeal to your audience—or at least, how not to offend them visually.

Make it a habit to ask customers for letters of recommendation on their own stationery. The price is right, and they are impressive, credible, and work wonders.

Keep your price lists and contracts accurate and current. Write articles on relevant aspects of your business. Try to get them published and then email, mail, or hand out reprints. Even if they aren't published, lay them out editorial style and distribute them anyway.

Use both electronic and print catalogs when you have multiple products to sell. Use pamphlets to explain certain aspects or applications of your product or service. Along with articles, they can become the basis for a PR release entitled "Free Guide on how to..."

Newsletters are a great excuse to keep talking to your prospects and customers. However, they take considerable work. If you are going to do a newsletter, budget enough money and plan on it taking more time than you think, whether the newsletter is printed or emailed. Do it right, do it on schedule, and do it for prospects and customers—not just for your employees. In other words, make it worth reading and valuable, not just a puff piece on you and your products.

Wrap Up

Digitize all your print collateral. These days, your most important print piece may be your business cards. Make yours stand out.

Chapter 22: Database Marketing

Your customer list can be your most valuable asset.

Create one central database (called the "house list" in the direct marketing world) with all your customers and prospect data. Grow it, nurture it, and protect it. It is your exclusive, intellectual property. Your trade secret.

The database serves as your company's main mailing list, provides management with a powerful information tool, and acts as an information insurance policy. Make your field salespeople responsible for maintaining subsets of your central database (their customers and prospects) from their own computers.

Customer Relations Management (CRM) and database software programs make all this relatively easy and offer automatic update features. For example, field salespeople can upload data into the central database and automatically update any customer/prospect files they changed that day. The updating process can work in the opposite direction too, with the central database automatically feeding new leads to the appropriate salesperson's computer.

A current central database mitigates the risks of a salesperson quitting without turning over his/her customer files. Prospect and customer records contain sensitive and important information. This data could be worth a fortune to your competition. Don't take any chances. In no case should salespeople be able to access any customer/prospect data other than their own.

An up-to-date centralized customer/prospect list will pay for itself repeatedly. It's ideal for finding the right customers when you want to unload excess inventory, or when you want to notify everyone of price changes, delivery information, or new product availability. Segment your database so that you can create a targeted, personalized letter and email or fax it to the appropriate prospects and customers in minutes.

If you are trying to create your own house list from scratch, look first to your accounting and salespeople. Accounting records probably have a wealth of information, but, unfortunately, they weren't collected for marketing purposes. However, you will find order statistics, addresses, and telephone numbers; so at least it's a start.

Salespeople tend to be protective of their customer and prospect names, so you may have to pry the information from them. The responsibility for creating and maintaining the central database lies in the home office.

Selling online can have an immediate payoff. A central database allows salespeople to access data on the fly and refresh the customer's record immediately after a sales call. Additionally, the home office can become a central qualifying mechanism, providing salespeople with qualified leads, and optimizing their time.

In one sense, your house list is a big mailing list that's easily segmented and controlled. It eliminates the convoluted logistics of exchanging mailing information with your field salespeople. You may also be able to take advantage of better postage discounts by mailing from a central location.

New prospect entries should include the name, title, contact data, information requested, and lead source. Enter this into the central database and then forward it to the appropriate salesperson and sales manager.

Typically, the home office will respond to the prospect requests for information by mail or email. In some cases, however, a salesperson may want to use the request as a door opener and deliver the materials in person.

Broaden your reach with rented lists. List brokers can supply you with names, addresses, and contact information for both industrial and consumer buyers. With just a few keystrokes, you can size your market (or potential market), determine major account locations, and initiate a direct response (email, mail, and telemarketing) program.

A typical industrial record includes the CEO's name, the major department heads, company address, telephone numbers, size (number of employees, annual sales), ownership (public/private), year started, type of site (headquarters, branch, single location), and type of business.

Wrap Up

Not only does your customer list identify your best prospects for future sales, it's also what prospective investors in your company look at seriously.

SELLING

Chapter 23: The Sales Process

There is no greater advantage than being there when the customer is ready to buy.

- Larry Lummis
My first sales manager, mentor, and friend

Make sure everybody involved in your sales and marketing plans understands your standard procedures regarding pricing, terms, conditions, and credit. Start with definitions so that everyone is speaking the same language. Next determine who is responsible for what.

Orders, Backlog, Sales

A sale and an order are not the same thing. To one person a sale may mean an order; to another it might be a shipment or a collection. Sales are different from orders.

An order is a signed contract that commits the buyer to accept and pay for a product or service. If a new order has been received from a customer you've never done business with before, it is sometimes prudent to book (count in your backlog) only those portions of the order that are not easily canceled.

Be suspicious of orders that commit the customer to deliveries for a long period of time; book only that portion of a large order that can be shipped and invoiced in the foreseeable future. You may, for example, want to make your definition of a bookable order one that is deliverable in the next 60 or 90 days.

Backlog consists of booked orders that have not yet shipped.

A sale is defined as a shipment to the customer with an accompanying invoice. Any sale contingent on special acceptance terms should not be counted until the special terms are satisfied.

What is *your* definition of an order? When does an order turn into a sale? What criteria must be met before an order can be booked and counted in the backlog? Write your definitions in a chart. When you're happy with them, formally document them and make them mandatory reading and reference material for everyone in your organization.

Therefore, formally define your criteria for an order. Determine factors such as, does an order requesting delivery in six months and/or with some sort of contingency get counted alongside orders that will get delivered next week?

Pricing, Terms and Conditions

Pricing strategy is dictated by your business model and, of course, the market. Your price list must be understandable with clear, easy to read descriptions of exactly what will be delivered, its price, and any prerequisites. Discounting must be standard. Only select personnel may offer special pricing. Since special pricing can have future ramifications, think beyond the deal at hand and consider how this will affect future orders with this customer.

Insist on *quid pro quo* as a condition of making concessions. In other words, if you lower your price, request early payment, a shorter warranty period, or a longer-term commitment. Make sure you get something in return.

Regarding payment terms and conditions, until the check clears, or your bank records the electronic transfer, all you have is a promise to pay. The time it takes to collect is a major factor in business success. Don't treat this lightly. Make it a standard, irrevocable policy that you send all invoices either with the sale or within hours after the sale. Don't wait until the invoice is due to start asking for your money. Plan for returns and refunds. Create a separate account for planned bad debts.

Extending payment terms to the wrong people can put you out of business. Cash in advance or COD is an excellent credit policy for new accounts. Then, establish a small credit limit and gradually increase the limit as the account proves to be credit worthy. Under what conditions will you offer payment terms? Can you really afford to do this?

Lastly, and most importantly, make it an irrevocable rule that you will not ship to any account that has past due invoices. Inform your customers about this right from the start. You must enforce this rule.

Here's why: All business experience cash flow problems. Your business is no exception. Not having enough cash on hand to pay the bills on time is a way of life for many firms. Invoices that get paid go to companies that (1) are insistent about payment and (2) will no longer ship goods unless old invoices are satisfied. Make these your company's policies.

Wrap Up

A Standard Operating Instruction manual will help make processes related to sales run smoothly. You need clarity and buy in as you put together a sales plan.

Chapter 24: The Sales Plan

The more doors I knock on, the more sales I make. A more eloquent way of saying this comes from *Forbes* publisher Rich Karlgaard:

> *Salespeople who make more sales calls will almost always outperform those making fewer calls. However, there is more to it than the mathematics of making more calls raises the chances of success. Frequent callers put themselves on a faster learning curve. They discover more quickly what works, what doesn't. They're quicker to learn techniques to overcome objections. Double the number of calls and sales will more than double. The act of making lots of calls also helps a person learn self-discipline and understand the rewards of delayed gratification.*
>
> \- (Karlgaard, Rick, "Smarts in Business is Not About IQ," *Forbes*, 16 December 2013)

Sales plans establish orders and sales goals by category: for example, product line, new/repeat business, territory, account, and, almost always, persons responsible.

Once sales goals have been determined, you'll need to calculate your prospecting requirements. How many cold calls, telephone calls, letters, and meetings will you need to make your orders goal?

Tracking orders received is the simplest way to measure the effectiveness of your salespeople. This is because salespeople may or may not have direct responsibility for product/service delivery or payment but are always responsible for booking orders.

Sales lag orders, so sales goals must reflect the time required to turn an order into a sale. And, of course, collections lag sales.

Make sure the orders/sales goals you assign are slightly higher that the number you really need to make a profit. This way if the sales organization falls short of quota, the company can still make a profit.

Goals by Product Line

For each major product line, what are the orders, sales, and collections goals?

Order Quotas. Who is responsible for bringing in orders? Quotas should be ambitious yet attainable. Set them too high and everyone may become discouraged; too low and you have planned on and settled for mediocrity.

Divide your overall orders goal across your sales channels. Leave some room for error. Make sure that the sum of all the individual goals exceeds the overall goal by 10 to 20 percent.

For example, if your orders goal is $100,000 and you have four equal size dealers, each dealer's goal should be between $27,500 (10 percent above) and $30,000 (20 percent above). Offer an incentive if they make the $30,000.

Distribute your orders goals as it makes sense for your organization. The easiest way is by salesperson, reseller/store, or by territory/account. Keep it simple.

Repeat versus new account business. New orders come from new accounts. Repeat orders are just that—follow-on orders from old customers. Your total orders goal equals your new orders goal plus your repeat orders goal.

For each orders quota, what is the planned mix of repeat versus new orders? Consider paying extra commissions on new account business. Plan for some order cancellations.

Qualified prospects. What's your definition? What criteria must an opportunity meet before you consider it a viable prospect? The chart below should help you formulate your policy.

Your company's new opportunity qualification criteria
Fit. Can your product solve their problem? Is it a good choice for them?
Money. Do they have the budget to make a purchase?
Schedule. How soon from now should they be planning on purchasing?
Commitment. How important is it that they make a purchase in the planned time frame? Why couldn't they put it off until next quarter?
Authorization. Does your contact have the authority to buy? Who else is involved in the purchase decision?
Qualified vendor. Does your company meet the purchasing company's criteria for an authorized vendor?
Familiarity. Have you done business with this customer previously? If no, why not?
Competition. Is there some reason why they would choose a competitor and not you? What can you do about that?

Finding qualified prospects

How many new qualified prospects Marketing Qualified Leads (MQL) and Sales Qualified Leads (SQL) will you need each month to make your new orders goal? Let's size up the challenge and determine how many new prospects you are going to need.

How many qualified new prospects must you uncover each month?	
Explanation	Elaboration
Step 1. Estimate your average sales price (ASP) from each customer. For example, if you sell $4,000 worth of products to 100 people, the average sales price is $40.	This is your Average Sales Price
Step 2. What are your new orders goal each month?	Your monthly new orders goal
Step 3. Divide your ASP (step 1) into the orders goal (step 2). The result tells you how many new customer orders you need to make orders goal.	# of new customers required each month to make the new orders goal.
Step 4. When you find someone who qualified to buy (from you or your competitor), on average how often will you win the order from that qualified prospect? Seven out of ten times (70%), one in two (50%), one in three (33%), and so on?	% of qualified prospects that buy from you
Step 5. Divide your number of new customers required each month (step 3) by the percent of qualified prospects that buy from you (step 4). The result is the number of new qualified prospects you need each month to make the orders goal	# of new, qualified prospects required each month to make your new orders goal

Efficiency

The next step is figuring out how well each of your prospecting methods works. For each approach, estimate the percentage that uncovers qualified buyers. In other words, if four of every hundred telephone calls yield a qualified prospect, your phone call efficiency is 4 percent.

Do the same for each of your prospecting methods.

Prospecting Method Efficiency
Telephone. Percent of qualified prospects per 100 prospecting calls
Direct Mail. Percent of qualified prospects per mailing to new prospects
Advertising. Percent of qualified buyers per number of ad responses
Cold Calls. Percent of qualified buyers per 10 calls
Other

Contacts

You can talk forever about strategies and plans, but you still must beat the bushes to find enough prospects to meet your new orders goal. So, now let's determine how many phone calls, letters, ads, or cold calls you are going to have to make to meet your new orders goals.

First, go back to the Step 5 of the "Qualified New Prospects" table and note the number of new qualified prospects you need to make your new monthly new account orders goal.

Now, using the efficiency chart, you can determine how many phone calls, and/or cold calls you will have to execute to uncover enough qualified prospects to meet your new customer orders goals.

Accountability

When you lose and don't get the sale, ask why. Often you can learn more about what matters by interviewing those people who decided to buy from your competitors. Another way to gain insight on what's really happening is to call up the competitor's salesperson who won the deal. Give congratulations, invite him/her to meet with you personally. Salespeople love to talk, especially when it's about themselves. You'll learn more than you imagined.

Target Accounts

In the Markets chapter, you determined which markets made the most sense for you to pursue. Now you are going to get more specific and identify the actual accounts you're going to go after within those markets. These are important choices, so before you write serious individual target account plans, visit some of these accounts and get a sense of how difficult it's going to be to make something happen there. This way you're not just going down a list and making decisions without first-hand experience.

- Go where your competitors do not have their heavy artillery in place.
- Where you fit, where the deck isn't stacked against you (ideally in a market that is just emerging) and of course in a market and accounts where you can get in and get a qualified audience.

If, however, you (or your boss) wants you to go after your competitor's biggest account, make certain your product really fits in that account, offers that customer real value and you have a compelling sales story. If it doesn't, look for easier pickings. Coming in second in a battle for the big one is worse than coming in last. If, however, your product really does stand up to the competition in that account, go for it!

And always remember: Your product qualifies you to compete for the business. Your selling skills, however, are the ultimate differentiator. In other words, the difference between a win and a loss is, first, product fit and then, the salesperson.

"There is only one way to crack a target account—be there." That is what my first sales manager said when he ordered me to spend every Thursday morning in the lobby of a major target account (where the market leader excelled). My job was to phone people upstairs (cold call) and try and get someone to sign me in and hear what I had to say. Naturally, when I finally did get upstairs, the person was rarely qualified; however, I'd always ask if he could identify someone who might have more interest and if I could use his name as a reference.

Ultimately, I got to know lots of people there and then one day (months later), the phone rang. One of my new contacts told me their market-leader vendor was having trouble meeting his delivery requirements and asked if I could come in and talk to his boss. Being there really does pay off.

Target Account Data
What features and benefits of your line does this account need?
If they are using a competitive product, why?
How can you beat your competitor in this account? Many companies create Battle Cards for each competitor. These provide sales and marketing people with an overview of the competitor's products and services and offer guidelines on how to win business when selling against that competitor.
Where are your products weakest for this situation? What can you do about it?
Who are the key decision makers and influencers?
How can you make each of them aware of you and your product?
What are your sales messages and plans for each of them?
What could you do (creative/unusual) beyond the normal to capture your customer's attention and imagination?
Who do you know who could help you sell and win this account?
Are there any other applications or departments within the account where your product fits?

Wrap Up

- What are you orders goals (new + repeat = goal) by sales channel?

Performance versus goal needs to be public knowledge. Salespeople are natural competitors, post your daily/weekly results versus plan.

Chapter 25: The Sales Call

It's fine to celebrate success, but it's more important to heed the lessons of failure.

- Bill Gates
Microsoft Founder, Philanthropist

I decided to get into sales after years on the engineering side. Why not? Our products were very technical, and our buyers were engineers. They would love to have a salesman who really knew all the technical details. Or so I thought.

Many, many months later I was still looking for my first new account order. My boss finally sat me down and told that my long-winded, detailed presentations on how our products worked was driving him and our prospects crazy. He told me that the next time someone asked me how the products worked, I was forbidden to stand up, go to the white board, and give a non-stop talk on the technical secrets of our design. Instead, I was to remain seated and say something like, "Terrific. All our customers love it. If you place an order now, I can get you a preferred delivery spot. There is no finer product like this so your decision will be good for your company and your reputation."

Of course, he was right. The new approach changed the subject to buying and customer satisfaction and away from how things worked. That was one of my first of many sales and marketing lessons learned.

The sales call is the salesperson's moment of truth. You are there first to find out what it takes to make a deal and then to make one. To do this, you'll

1. Sell yourself. Get your prospect to want to do business with you (not necessarily with your company or product)
2. Understand your prospect's wants and needs.
3. Show how your product solves the prospect's problem.
4. Handle objections.
5. Close the sale.

All the above requires preparation, probing and listening, product knowledge and sales skills. People love to hear themselves talk. Listening makes you captivating. Listen to what is and isn't said. Listen with your eyes. Listening works. Listeners win.

Even though more and more business is now being conducted online, consumer research reveals customers still want a direct and personal relationship with their sellers. Take an extra few minutes to talk with your customers. Get to know them. People don't want their relationships to be a "fly by."

Time and Territory Management

Have you ever noticed that the best prospects are usually busy while the looky-loos, the people who like to talk about anything but buying and waste everyone's time, seem to have all the time in the world? That's probably why more than one successful salesperson has told me that that time-management skills are the basis of their superior performance.

Write down what you need to do every week, or even daily. Take five minutes to determine where you are and prioritize what you need to get done. Make a list. When you don't plan, it's easy to spend more time traveling than talking to prospects. Travel time is a killer—one of your biggest enemies. Confirm all meetings before you get into the car or on the plane. Make sure a face-to-face meeting is necessary. Perhaps a phone call or online face-to-face meeting will work even better. Customer Relationship Management (CRM) software is great for this.

Figure out a way to have your prospects come to see you. If you could avoid going to an office where you are in unfamiliar territory (translate: loss of location advantage), you sure would save a lot of time and probably have a much higher comfort level being on your home turf. In any case, don't drive for an hour to discover you forgot to bring everything you need. Incomplete sales calls undermine everything you have tried to set up in advance. They happen when you forget to bring the right documentation, are in too big of a hurry, don't pay attention to what the prospect says, or talk too much.

When I was working in engineering, I could get up and work very early or work very late. When I became a salesman, I realized that no one wanted to talk to me at 6 AM. If, however, if your prospect is up to it, a breakfast meeting really works. They lengthen your selling day and you get the prospect when he or she is the freshest, without interruptions. The real point, however, is you can't afford to do anything but sell during normal business hours. Do your paperwork and other non-selling activities some other time.

Take care of your existing customers. Current customers are almost always your most predictable source of new orders. Take the time to handle customer complaints. Anticipate them. Don't wait for your customers to call you. You call them. Look for problems. Customers appreciate this and it really makes a difference when they think about with whom they are going to place the next order. This doesn't mean you have to be there every minute, but it does mean that you must be on top of any problem and make sure your customer's problems get solved. Take care of your customers and they'll take care of you.

Finally, you can't afford to be without rejection.

If your prospect is qualified, then you make an appointment for a face-to-face meeting. So, what if your target always buys from the competition. Your job, your skill, is winning business from the competition. You'll win some and lose some. Rejection is part of the deal. Don't worry about it. Even the best lose regularly.

Qualifying Prospects

If your prospects are not qualified, you're wasting your time.

What's wrong with the 80 percent of the salespeople who underperform? Are they lazy, saying the wrong things, talking too much? Maybe. But if you put the "best" salesperson in front of an unqualified prospect and the "worst" salesperson in front of a qualified prospect, the "worst" will outsell the "best" every time.

What do the 20 percent do that the 80 percent don't? The top sellers qualify their prospects sooner. They spend most of their time with prospects who are interested in what they are selling, have enough money to afford it, and appear to be in a buying mood. Less productive salespeople don't qualify as quickly and spend too much time with unqualified buyers, that is, waste time trying to convince people who will never buy from them

In other words, the common denominator among good salespeople (the characteristic that is missing from the less effective salespeople) is the discipline to avoid wasting time with unqualified prospects. Instead they spend their valuable selling time with qualified prospects. People who want/need a product like theirs, can afford it, and have the authority and a schedule to make a purchase.

You've heard that some products sell themselves. Some almost do, and if you are ever fortunate enough to have such a product, get your salespeople to work double shifts and forget about lunch. The reality is that very few products are so visibly superior that they don't require expert marketing and selling. Make sure your product or service is clearly positioned, becauseyour product is the salesperson's first-level qualifier

What you sell determines if your prospect has interest. Your product enables your salespeople to compete for an order. In other words, a competitive product gets you into the race. Winning often has as much to do with the salesperson as the product. Many competitive situations are won by the best salesperson, and not necessarily the best product.

Poker, a game of luck and skill (like life) is a good example of how a good player (read: good salesperson) succeeds without the best hand (read: best product). Research of online poker matches reveals that less than 15 percent of all hands are won by players with the best hands. The rest all won by the players with the best story and most convincing behavior.

Product knowledge is your key to finding qualified prospects. If your most startling benefit, your product's unique selling proposition, leaves your prospect cold, then the salesperson is probably in the wrong place. More to the point, just because your prospect has money, a need to buy, and a schedule to purchase does not mean he or she is qualified. Your product must be able to satisfy your prospect's basic needs and the salesperson must see a way to win the business.

Sometimes you can be too smart, though. One of the wonderful things about youth and inexperience is that you really don't know when you're supposed to lose. If your salespeople know your product and believe it can make your prospect happy, they shouldn't necessarily abandon ship just because the prospect has your competitor's calendar on the wall and equipment in the next room. Have your salespeople start asking questions. Find out what turns this prospect on. Your product has given them a chance to compete. Now it's time for them to go to work and earn their keep. When you think about it, most products (yours and the competition) do what they claim.

It's up to the marketing department and the salesperson to make the difference in the mind of the prospect.

Wrap Up

- Life is too short to spend much selling time with unqualified prospects.
- Pay attention. Plan your call. What are the likely objections? What do you want to accomplish?
- Your goal is to find out what it takes to get an order. Talk less. Listen more.

Chapter 26: Influencers

People don't tend to make decisions by themselves.

Influencers are people who impact the sales process but don't purchase or use the product. Influencers can be those that prospects interact with personally and trust their opinion (family members, friends, colleagues, and others). Influencers in social media are people who have built a solid reputation, authority, and a substantial number of followers within a particular industry or around a specific subject.

Decision makers are surrounded by downward, lateral, and upward influencers and recommenders. Prospects rely on influencers to help them make decisions. Therefore, influencers are important because:

- Influencers have the power to quickly sway decision making and build awareness for products and/or a brand
- Without influencers you may have to spend a significant portion of your sales and marketing resources reaching out and selling to prospects
- Having the endorsement of a trusted acquaintance (or social influencer can provide instant credibility and increased sales rates.

When selling to consumers identifying the influencers is straightforward. A stereotypical example is a man (purchaser) who needs to add to his wardrobe. At the men's store, the spouse (influencer) will steer him away from what the "young guys are wearing at the office" to the dark blue suit.

When selling to companies it takes a little more work to identify the influencers. Who are the individuals and organizations that influence your customer? Selling to companies can be complicated. In industrial business-to-business sales there are typically three to five people involved in the buying decision. To determine the powers of influence, you need to understand how these companies work. Here are some of the roles people play in the buying process:

- Initiator. Who (and what department) initiates the buying process?
- Researcher. Who influences the type of product to be bought? Who investigates the different ways of solving the problem without specifying a certain vendor?
- Specifier. Who writes the specifications for the purchase?
- Short lister. Who determines which vendors will be asked to submit bids?
- Selector. Who makes the actual, final selection of product and supplier?
- Quantifier. Who decides on order size, delivery, payment terms, etc.?
- Signer. Who signs the order?
- Veto. Who has the power to veto the choice of product and supplier?

Entire departments can also be influential in the buying process. Think about the typical company you will be selling to and determine which organizations are most influential in selecting your product. To make this manageable and doable, simplify it down to three areas: top management, the department that will use your product, and the purchasing department.

What can you do to make these people want to recommend that their firm do business with you? What evidence or documentation do you have to support your claims? Top management, for example, may want references. Financial types will want comparative pricing, and people on the manufacturing side will want reliability data.

When seeking to find social influencers first make sure you fully define your target market since those are who you're trying to influence. Next, research where you can find the right influencers. There are many free and paid online tools such as moz.com/followerwonk/bio/ and buzzsumo.com that can help you target the right influencers. Once you've identified some influencers, begin to follow them on social media so you can better understand their activity and perhaps (tactfully) comment on posts, blogs and participate in other online conversations they're involved in. If there are industry events or conventions that the influencer is attending, this could be a great opportunity to personally meet them and form an authentic connection.

Wrap Up

- In determining a corporate influencer, start with the purchasing department.
- Ask your prospect who else should you be covering.
- Build relationships with the social influencers that matter to your business.

Chapter 27: Bonding with Prospects

The primary purpose of a typical sales call is to uncover what it takes for the customer to say "yes." That's why active listening—listening with your whole body—is an essential ingredient in bonding with your prospects. How else are you going to find out what will make the customer say "yes"?

Anticipate how your prospects are going to react to your sales call. Put yourself in their shoes. Imagine yourself as the buyer. If you were in the buyer's situation, what would you want from the salesperson, or the product or the vendor that would stimulate you to buy?

Prospects will feel good about themselves and want to buy when they:

- **Trust you.** People buy from people they trust and have a degree of comfort with. If they like you, that's even better. It is easier to like someone who listens to you and demonstrates respect than it is to like someone who talks at you most of the time. It's also easy to like and trust someone who has a pleasing appearance, exudes confidence, and does not waste your time.
- **Are confident your product can do the job.** If you were this buyer, what product, service, business issues would you be most interested in? List the features/benefits you

think will be most relevant to this person. What evidence/ demonstrations will you use to prove your points?

- **Know that other smart people are also buying your product.** Make sure your prospect knows that others believe your product is a smart buy. Tell your prospect how others have benefited.
- **Believe your company will stand behind the product.** Rave about your services. Tell a story. Cite examples.
- **Feel they are getting a bargain.** Make sure they know they are getting the best product at the best possible price. They want to believe this, so (1) make sure they are and (2) make sure you tell them they are.

All the points mentioned above center on building rapport, or bonding, with your prospect. In Body Language Sales Secrets, Jim McCormick offers physical ways to reinforce the rapport you are building with your prospect. Primarily, use open body language, which he describes as "actions and facial expressions that are invitational; they show a desire to connect and suggest that trust is present." (Body Language Sales Secrets, Career Press, 2018; p. 42)

Examples of open body language are:

- A smile with the eyes engaged. That means you'll see some wrinkles around the eyes.
- Movements that include open palms and arms comfortably away from the body rather than shielding it.
- Head nods and attentive eye contact that encourages continued conversation.
- Minimal or no reliance on self-soothing gestures such as rubbing hands together; there is a sense of calm in the conversation.

- Minimal or no barriers between you and the other person. There is a sense of easy interaction that makes barriers unnecessary.

Reinforce the rapport you are building even more by telling relevant stories. People really do buy for personal reasons. They want to know what's in it for them. People also tend to buy emotionally and later justify the purchase with logic, so anticipate what's going to be on your prospect's mind. If you think you'll need samples or evidence, make sure you bring them with you.

Your product enables you to compete, but after that, it's up to you to make them want to do business with you.

Keep in mind that the first twenty seconds of an encounter often determine if you will be taken seriously. Before meeting with your prospect, take a minute to visualize how you want the call to go and what you hope to achieve.

Look like you belong. Your dress and nonverbal selling skills can be just as important as what you say. Do not flop down in a chair and make yourself comfortable. Carry yourself well and use the open body language described above.

And no matter how worn out you might be going from call to call, be enthusiastic. If you don't get excited about your product, why should your prospect? Everyone likes to be around genuinely enthusiastic people, and no one likes to be around phonies. That said, make sure your energy level is appropriate for the person. If your meeting involves a reserved individual, you need to express your enthusiasm in a way that draws the person toward you rather than scares him to death. Make sure your brand of enthusiasm includes a smile; it's contagious.

For some people, like me, pretending I am being videotaped helps churn up my enthusiasm prior to a meeting. For others, visualization works better. Recall a similar situation where you were successful. Remember how good you felt when you finished that successful call. Now start the sales call that same positive, winning feeling.

Self-confidence really shows in this kind of situation. Try and act like you really have more than one prospect in the world. Nobody wants to do business with a hungry (desperate) salesperson.

Stay calm. After all, your purpose in being there is to show the prospect how to get something they want, and, to get it for them now. You are there to help them buy something that will make them happy. You are there to solve their problem.

One study of salespeople, where hundreds of actual sales calls were recorded on video tape, revealed that the first thing that struck everyone when they looked at the tapes was that the best salespeople were calmer than the others.

When I first became a sales manager and started going out with my salespeople, I was appalled at how much they talked and how little they listened. The prospect would start talking and my salesperson would interrupt. Think about that. Your job is to find out what it takes to get an order and you're going to interrupt the only person who knows the answer. As the Greek philosopher Epictetus said, "We have two ears and one mouth so that we can listen twice as much as we speak."

Some prospects ask potential vendors to make a formal presentation to a committee charged with making a buying recommendation. If that's the situation, do your best to be last. People recall and use the most recent information the most. Last impressions last.

The Warm-Up Process

Just because you're ready to do business doesn't mean that your prospect is. To achieve your mission, you'll need your prospect's undivided attention. Without preoccupied thoughts. Without distractions.

In order, your priorities are 1) sell yourself, 2) sell your company, and 3) sell your product. You are not selling price, as important as it may be.

In the paragraphs above, I offered you skill sets that help you sell yourself. What follows here involves use of all of them, and then builds on those skills so you can sell your company and your product.

People appreciate knowing that you know their name, so memorize names and be congenial. If this is a cold call, then state who you are, your firm, your product, and your intentions. If your opening remarks do not pique your prospect's interest, then you might have to jolt the prospect into paying attention. Find ways to elicit key questions from your prospect. They are generally something like, "How can you do that?" or "How is that possible?"

To evoke questions that help you establish a conversation, rather than a pitch, try leading with your most relevant benefit. For example,

- Our product can cut your printing costs by 25 percent.
- With our company you won't have to carry any inventory.
- Now you can get high-resolution color graphics at no extra cost.
- In ten minutes, you'll read faster and remember more.

If your prospect still won't pay attention, try something outlandish like asking him for an order. Say, "John, you seem awfully busy today, why don't you just go ahead and order my product, I'll take care of the details." At least three good things might happen: (1) John might enjoy your humor and warm up to you, (2) John might even order or (3) he may sit up and pay attention.

A more likely approach is to change the scenery. Take him to the cafeteria, to a restaurant, to a conference room, for a walk. Maybe you must reschedule your appointment. If getting his attention becomes too difficult, validate his interest and your understanding of his need. Maybe your prospect really isn't interested or is simply not qualified.

Driving Forward

Once the conversation starts getting serious, it's time to uncover the prospect's real buying motive(s). People buy for lots of reasons, usually personal (see the chapter on Behavioral Economics). Advertising agencies often write ads for the person the target customers imagine themselves to be, for example, showing a young, virile man driving a Corvette when the target buyer is a middle-age guy who can afford one.

Plan your approach. If you think you can wing it, you're wrong. Starting with your most startling benefit makes sense. Do it naturally without theatrics. Or try coaxing the prospect toward where you are the strongest. Don't overdo it, otherwise you may spend all your time explaining what you mean. You'll never be asked to prove an understatement. If you are using visual aids, then paint a visual image—scene in which the prospect is enjoying or using the product.

As you cultivate a rapport with the person, it will become easier for you to uncovering what that prospect really wants. You want to find out (1) what would keep this person from buying and (2) what will make this person want to buy. Stimulate your prospect to react to each feature or benefit, first presenting your information or feature, following up with the benefit, and then a question.

Information: "Our product includes the latest ..."

Benefit: "You'll get your work done in 25 percent less time.

Question: "How important would a 25 percent-time savings be to you?"

This process encourages the prospect to talk even more. Answer each question with another question such as "Why?" Then go on to your next point: information, benefit, question. Get your prospect's reaction. The longer the person's talks and the less you talk the better you are doing. So, when customers tell you they are looking for "real value" or the "best return on investment," probe a little deeper.

Try using four simple words like "In addition to that [what else are you looking for]" to determine if the reason offered by your prospect is real or just sounds good. And when you finally get an answer that's a little more personal and closer to home, ask "why." What's happening is you're homing in on what really matters.

You'll find that the longer it takes for people to tell you what they really want, the less likely they are to buy. That's because people really don't buy things; they buy how its described and how it affects them personally. So, once you think you've uncovered this prospect's key issue, stop!

Try a trial close. If you're not sure you can satisfy that critical need today, try a "Just suppose" close. You say, "Just suppose we can meet your critical requirement, when could we expect an order?"

Don't be surprised when you discover that your customer is not buying for the "right" reasons. People generally have two reasons for buying: one that sounds good (politically correct) and a real one.

No matter what the prospect says he or she wants, your answer that invites an outpouring of detail— "in addition to that what would make you happy"—is one of the most powerful questions in selling.

Almost There

We've devoted the next chapter to the close, but here are considerations that are critical to your success as you move through the sales process.

Objections

Selling doesn't really start until the prospect says, "No." Keep asking questions. You're probing to find out what's keeping you from getting an order. Nothing else matters. Stop talking about what you and the prospect agree upon and concentrate instead on what's in the way of making a sale. When you start to notice the reactions becoming a little more emotional, you're probably getting close to uncovering the real issues.

Objections are signposts to an order. Hear the objection out. Let the prospect talk without interruption. Your prospect may keep right on talking and get to the real issue. Don't handle every objection. Ignore subjective comments and hypothetical issues. Some salespeople swear they won't handle any objection until they hear it twice. Formal studies of salespeople in action reveal that the best salespeople only responded to real objections. Whereas the less effective salespeople spent most of their time responding to the least important questions and trying to prove the wrong points.

When I first got into sales management, I couldn't believe how often the poorer salespeople were constantly responding, in detail, to every question. They were treating all questions and objections with equality and missing the buying signals. The conversation needs to focus on what's keeping the prospect from placing order.

Treat the objection as a request for more evidence.

"Your product is outdated; I want something more contemporary." Turn this objection around so that you are responding to, "Show me how your product compares with some of the newer products in the market."

"I have to talk this over with my supervisor." Respond as though the prospect said, "Give me more information so that I can buy without another opinion."

Use exhibits, demonstrations, and statistics for the logical, analytical types. Use testimonials and stories for the more emotional, talker types.

Try the "feel, felt, found method" in the face of objections. Your prospect says, "I would rather keep using my old system, at least I know how to use it and I won't be wasting time learning a new one."

You respond with... I certainly understand how you **feel**. Nobody likes to take the time to learn a new system. Several of our customers **felt** the same way. However, once they tried our new product, they **found** the brief time it took to learn the new system saved them hours every week.

Know your competition

You can often tell how you are doing by the nature of the objections, which sometimes include references to your competition. If you start to hear questions that ask about features that are your competitor's strengths, then beware, your competitor is influencing how your prospect is thinking.

For all your relevant competitors, you should know at a minimum their (1) unique selling propositions and have a canned response for it and (2) those features of your product or service that put each competitor on the defensive. So, handle the objections quickly and crisply, and then move the conversation toward those areas where you are strongest.

Recycled, but Relevant Pushback

For every product, there are certain criticisms that just about all prospects raise. Your salespeople should have been trained to have stock answers for these.

- **Price.** "Your price is too high."
- **Missing or competitive features.** "I need such-and-such a feature (a feature you don't have or one that the competition touts.)."
- **Service.** "What do I do if the product doesn't work?"
- **Credibility.** "How can I be sure your company is financially strong enough to provide me with the support I'll need?"
- **References.** "I would like to talk to some of your customers who are trying to do what I am planning to do with your product."

Handling excruciating details

Nowhere do details count more than when dealing with local, state, or federal government agencies. I would be remiss if I didn't share what happened to a client of mine, a small, minority-owned manufacturing company. They spent months designing and configuring a set of equipment designed to meet California's rigorous traffic safety requirements.

The state then requested proposals for that type of equipment. The bidding form stated that if you are offering fully compliant equipment, check the "Yes" box and fill in a price. We the manufacturer checked "Yes," bid a low, what should be a winning price, and then to make sure the state understood just how compliant our offer really was, added a sentence stating, "The equipment proposed is equivalent to the state's XYZ part number [a part number the state had assigned to our product they had previously purchased from us for evaluation purposes (and loved it). So instead of just saying yes, we added more information. At the bid opening, ours was the lowest (winning) price.

I called a few days later to inquire when we could expect a purchase order. Instead I was informed that our apparent winning bid was thrown out. Why? Because they had no record of a XYZ product. Turns out, we made a typing error and transposed two of the digits in the referenced part number. At a protest meeting it was determined the state had no obligation to look beyond the surface of the bid. Imagine, months of work negated because of extra unwanted information and one typo.

If paying attention to the details is not your forte, then hire someone to be your watchdog. Make sure they can add. You can't imagine how many times an arithmetic error results in products and services being offered at the wrong price. Naturally, it always seems to work to your disadvantage. If the error results in too high a price, you lose the deal. Make the mistake the other way and you end up with less profit or a loss.

Have at least two people check the arithmetic and forms (to ensure they are filled out correctly). It is not unusual to have 25 percent or more of all the bidders for public sector solicitations be disqualified because they didn't check all the boxes or completely answer some obscure question or added some confusing information.

Also, talk to the buyer before the bids are due. Ask questions. Make sure you understand their evaluation criteria, for example, does a prompt-pay discount count toward determining low bidder?

And, if after all this, you still make a major mistake, call the buyer. He/she may be sympathetic and help you avoid a catastrophe.

Know Your Types

Although you do not want to pigeonhole someone you've just met, slipping your prospects into basic categories can help you stay on track in talking with them. Here are a few; feel free to redefine or add your own based on experience.

- **The Talker.** Likes people. Worries how people will react to the product. Wants to please others. Likes to talk about kids, hobbies, and personal things.

  Use questions such as, "Who else will be involved using the product?" and "What do these people think about this product?"

- **The Entrepreneur.** Business like. No small talk. Impulsive, tends to make gut decisions as soon as he thinks he has all the facts. Doesn't talk detail; talks results.

  Will respond to questions about his/her work or achievements: "How can we save time? and "What sort of payoff are you looking for?"

- **The Analyst.** Wants details. May be less interested in getting the job done and more interested in how it works. Logical, no nonsense type; low on people skills.

Try questions such as "How would you rate our product?" and "How do you keep so well organized?"

One last comment that repeats an essential point made above. It's tough to get someone to say yes if they don't like you. Keep them talking. Most people love the sound and wisdom in their own voice. Make them feel important and comfortable. They'll think you're the greatest!

Wrap Up

You are selling yourself—always keep that in mind. After that, what problem will you, your company or your product solve in the life of your customer? If this customer decides in your favor, what's in it for him/her personally? Status, recognition?

Since almost all prospects prefer to talk, you listen.

- **Listen** to their answers.
- **Pause** before you answer (he or she may keep right on talking and get to the real reason).
- **Don't interrupt** even if you know what they are going to say.
- **Use silence** to encourage your prospect to talk.
- **Repeat back what you heard**; show you understand.
- **Don't settle** for the first response. Instead answer with "In addition to that?" or "Why?"

Chapter 28: Closing

Ask for the order and shut up.

Silence is the most effective form of pressure. Asking for an order should appear to come naturally in the process of a sales call. The key to this, however, is after asking for the order, having the discipline to stop talking.

Think of it this way. After you ask for the order, the next person who talks is at a disadvantage. By forcing your prospect to talk, you're either going to win, lose or find out what is keeping you from winning.

There is more than one way to ask for an order and, to some extent it depends on the quality of the rapport you have with the customer. Another factor, of course, is how well you sold the company and the product after you sold yourself. Some of these may seem abrupt when you read them, but tone of voice and context make all the difference in the world as to how effective they are:

- **Trial close.** The client says, "I wish we could afford one of those." You respond, "If we could meet your budget constraints, when could we expect an order?"
- **Approach close.** You say, "When I am finished all I ask is that you tell me if my product applies to your situation." Another example is, "If I could show you the best laser printer in the market, could you spend $1,000 to try it out?"

- **Power of suggestion close.** "Picture yourself with this beautiful ..."
- **Just suppose close.** Prospect says, "I can only use your product if it is less than nine inches wide." You say, "Just suppose we could do that, could we have an order by...?"
- **Closing on an objection.** "Will you buy if we meet your specification?"
- **"Say what?" close.** The prospect says, "I can't afford it." You now jolt the prospect into paying attention by saying, "That's exactly why you should buy it now. The prospect says, "What?" You say, "You and I both know you are going to buy a product like this eventually. This product will never be cheaper than it is today, and it will start saving you money immediately.
- **Another "Say what?" close.** The prospect says, "I'm not interested. You say, "I didn't think you would be." The prospect says, "What?" You say, "Almost everyone reacts that way. First, they say they're not interested. However, once they try it, most become satisfied customers."
- **Change places close.** You say, trying to get the prospect to tell you the real reason that is keeping him from buying, "Put yourself in my situation, I have given you all you need to know to buy my product and we're still at an impasse." Ideally the prospect says, "Well this is my real concern" and then provides what he sees as a door-closing objection. However, the prospect may not respond, so it's your turn to speak: "It's the money isn't it?" (or whatever you really think is keeping you from an order).
- **Assumptive close.** "How will you be paying for the product?" or "If you would like, I will arrange for overnight delivery."

- **Either/or close.** "Will you want to order with or without the optional...?"
- **Direct close.** "When can I expect a purchase order?" Or "I would like to stop by on Friday and pick up a check."

Wrap Up

Ask for the order, then be quiet.

Chapter 29: Repeat Business

You cannot afford to oversell—to exaggerate benefits and overstate results. That's because, while new account business is the foundation for growth, repeat account business is the foundation for profitability. Getting the order is not the end of the business relationship; it is the beginning.

As the sale nears a climax, you may find yourself selling less and negotiating more. Overselling is usually worse than not making a sale at all, so don't make promises you may not be able to keep, because if you do, you will soon regret it. Repeat business is the most predictable and reliable way to keep the cash wheel spinning.

When the customer says "yes," don't treat it like a rare event.

Stay in control of yourself. This is no time to be effusive. Remember, an order should be a mutually profitable transaction. The customer has neither given nor received a favor. Both parties have responsibilities.

Getting that "yes," is great time to start selling more products or services, that is, once customers decide to buy, they are significantly more likely to say yes to subsequent offers. You see this in retail all the time, when the clerk suggests companion products to complement the item you're purchasing.

We used this very effectively with a mail-order cataloger I once worked with. First, on the telephone, the salesperson would always follow the customer's request to purchase with "How many" and

"And what else." "Add another product to your order now and we'll include it in the same package. You'll save on shipping."

Once the order was finalized, they would immediately follow with an email or post-card acknowledgment. The mail confirmed the order, identified a delivery date, and made a "special" offer. The "special" was a product that was either a complimentary product (at a great price) or an excess inventory item (also at a great price). The offer stipulated that they could only buy at this price if they ordered in time for the special to ship with the original order.

How well did it all work? The telephone "upgrade and/or cross sale" really worked well and increased the average sales prices substantially and that the "special" email/postcard added about 5 percent to the firm's revenue. That's a 5 percent revenue increase without any incremental sales or marketing costs (other than an email or post card).

We once determined that without the incremental revenues from the telephone upgrades, the follow- up mail and some special promotions, the company would have been barely profitable.

Sustaining the Bond

Set up a procedure to ensure follow up with every new customer. The goal is to build on that relationship that started with the first sale. Introduce the customer to the rest of your products and the kinds of services that are available. Show that you and your company care. Your objective is to turn new customers into perpetual ones.

Anticipate problems

There are always problems. Rather than wait for your customers to call with problems, call them up. Go visit them. Look for problems. This way, everybody wins. Not only will you build the right relationship with the customer, you'll also uncover new needs, and new opportunities to make more sales.

Above all, save their names and addresses. It was always negligent not to maintain an accurate customer list. Today, it would be insanity considering computers, Customer Relationship Management (CRM) and on-line databases.

Customer Service

Serious customer service calls almost always involve the salesperson (and if they don't, they should). Here are some basic truths to effective customer service:

- You are better off disappointing customers with the truth than to satisfy customers temporarily with a lie.
- Don't hurry problem customers off the phone. Let them decide when they are finished. Let them talk and vent their anger or frustrations. Customers always appreciate sensitivity and responsiveness.
- Fast response can overcome lots of sins. Make sure the problem stays fixed by following up after the service is rendered.

Wrap Up

Stay in contact with your customer. Look for problems.

Chapter 30: Sales Management

There are only three ways to increase and grow revenues:

- More customers
- Larger average order size (buy more and/or pay higher prices)
- Customer purchases more often

Sales Staff

There is one primary way to enable you to accomplish those three: hiring great sales professionals and managing them well. In a way, managing salespeople is like managing professional athletes. Successful sports team managers hire the best players they can afford, put them into situations where they are most likely to succeed, measure results, cut their losses quickly and are constantly looking for new and better players.

Please note what successful managers don't do. They typically do not bring in players who have never played the position they want to fill. They do not try to train someone to pitch who's never pitched before. Nor do they procrastinate when the player is unable to perform as needed. Of course, there are exceptions to the above, but the fundamental idea is sound. Hiring the most qualified people is the sales manager's most important job. Sales is where the 80/20 rule prevails. Do whatever it takes to find those 20 percenters who will make the most sales, make you the most money and keep you employed.

Hire salespeople who already know (or can quickly learn) how to sell products like yours Advertise for the best people; for example, if the sales position pays between $75,000 and $150,000 depending on performance, but in extraordinary cases a sales person could earn $250,000, advertise "Make up to $250,000".

Beware, good salespeople are natural interviewees. Even marginal performers often interview well. Here's an interview technique that you, the interviewer, can use to quickly reveal which of your candidates are right for your situation.

Instead of basing your hiring decision on how well your candidates answer questions, have them role play and try to sell you something, preferably your own product. For example, if you sell office supplies, early in the interview tell your candidate you would like to spend the next couple of minutes doing a role play. Then hand him a yellow wooden pencil and inform him that you want to buy ten thousand of them. "So," you tell him, "take two minutes, right now, and plan on how you're going to sell me those pencils."

Then be silent. Do something at your desk or stand-up and walk away while he thinks out a strategy. Sit back down and start the role play by saying, "Mr. Jones, I understand you sell pencils." What happens next is up to him. This technique lets you see first-hand how your candidate performs under pressure while doing the very work you are hiring him to perform.

Note that this approach works better if you sell something more complicated than pencils. For example, hand your candidate a one-page description of one of your more complicated products. Make sure the document identifies a major feature/benefit or two. Provide him with a quiet spot and about ten minutes to figure out what it is he is selling. Then have him come back into your office and try to sell you one or many, whatever makes sense.

As he's trying to sell you, ask him about those features in the document. Not only will you get a chance to measure his selling skills and how he responds under pressure, you also get a chance to test his ability to understand and communicate technical/product features that will be critical to his success. In short, hire smart, pleasant people—people with integrity who will win business legitimately—and help them become product experts as you motivate them to succeed.

Training

Spending lots of money training salespeople can be a waste, but it depends the type of training, the quality of the trainer, and the needs of the team. I have a friend who sometimes does body language training with salespeople, but it's no more than 90 minutes rather than the investment of a whole day. Her focus is primarily self-awareness, so the sales pros have an improved sense of their own nervous gestures, vocal changes under stress, and other basics such as the open body language I mentioned before.

In hard-skills training, as opposed to soft-skills training like body language, limit your initial training investment to showing your new salespeople where to prospect, how to qualify, and what to say in the form of a "canned" pitch. Have them memorize the pitch and the answers to the most common objections. That's it. One week later, do the same thing with the same agenda and subject matter. Repetition works. Next week do it again until you are confident your company and product are being properly represented.

Don't get caught up with time-wasting "training" topics like company history, marketing theories, irrelevant product information, long-term objectives, and organizational structures.

Stay away from the nice-to-know and concentrate on the need-to-know, that is, only what your salespeople need to know to make sales. Take the rest of the money you were going to spend on training and use it on motivational and incentive programs. Augment the training with marketing campaigns that uncover prospects so well qualified, even untrained salespeople will be able to close them.

Motivation

People generally wanted to be treated with professional courtesy by their managers. They enjoy being coached and trained with patience and logic. And they really appreciate an understanding manager.

Salespeople are the same, but different. Sure, they like to be treated nicely. However, they and their managers, are interested in one thing only—sales. So, when it comes to managing salespeople, don't think for one minute you are dealing with accountants or engineers or clerks. You're dealing with a different species.

Salespeople live a different sort of life from most people. For one, they have an uneven existence—on the edge—continually experiencing highs and lows. At any given moment they may feel down and out after being told no too many times or given a hard time by a rude customer. The next moment they can be closing a big order and feeling on top of the world.

The other distinguishing characteristic of salespeople is that just about all of them are motivated by the same things—money, competition, and recognition. So, to keep your salespeople from jumping out of the window (or worse yet, not making quota), forget about appealing to their logic and reason.

Exploit their competitive nature. Keep your salespeople under constant pressure. That's right pressure. Stimulate them with daily goals. Drive them. Inspire them. Repetitive practice is what makes most people great and that includes selling. Your salespeople need to do the same correct things repeatedly.

Norman, a spectacularly successful entrepreneur, salesman and friend, is a real advocate of getting the right sales pitch and approach and using it repeatedly. He tells the story that as a kid, he grew up in the printing business cleaning presses, loading trucks, and doing all the dirty work. When he turned eighteen, he went to the owner and asked him if he could become a salesman for the company. The owner laughed and sent him back to clean the rest rooms.

Norm was not to be denied and continued to badger the owner for a chance to sell. Finally, the owner relented and let Norm try. On his first sales call he told the customer that this was his first day selling and he wanted to show the boss that he could really make sales, so "couldn't you at least try us out with an initial order for some envelopes or anything so I can prove myself to the boss."

It worked. He then used the line again and again until he couldn't get away with it anymore. As a teenager, he became the company's highest performing salesman. He then went on to own one of the largest printing companies in Southern California.

When it comes time to reward salespeople, make sure you do it in public, in front of their peers. One of the most successful sales managers I've ever met meets with his entire sales force every morning, six days a week. He sets goals, reviews result, praises the best, cajoles some, damns a few, and stimulates all.

He encourages competition. He even books bets between the salespeople and often makes bets himself, usually on the weaker performers (think about how smart a move that is).

He knows what makes salespeople tick and he drives them to peak performance. He's the consummate sales manager. He's also a multi-millionaire. That's because he knows that money, competition, and recognition are what salespeople are all about.

Manufacturer's Representatives

Manufacturers' representatives should already be calling on your target accounts and prospects. Reps are independent businesspeople manufacturers hire to sell their products. Reps make their living from commissions on sales they make and are not paid a salary or stipend.

As a rule, reps don't have time to make sales calls on companies or prospects who can only use one of their lines. Instead, they want to be able to sell every manufacturer's line they represent on every sales call. Thus, the representative's selling skills and industry knowledge are a lot less important than their current product lines and sales call patterns.

As a result, the most important criteria for selecting a manufacturer's representative is to choose one who has complimentary products to yours and is already calling on the kind of people who should be buying your products. It is very difficult, if not impossible, to get a manufacturer's representative to change their sales call patterns.

Wrap Up

- Never stop looking for new/better salespeople.
- You'll never regret spending more for the right person.

Chapter 31: Sales Forecasting

Predictability begets profitability.

Running and budgeting and growing an effective and profitable sales organization is highly dependent on how well future sales are forecast. A reasonably accurate forecast of sales and collections over the next, say quarter, is really the only way you can determine how much to spend and budget the entire operation.

Sales Forecasting. Don't leave it up to salesperson as to what percentage they apply to their account forecasts. Otherwise a 75 percent chance from one salesperson is really 50/50 at best and from another 75 percent is really 90 percent. Have documented, absolute requirements for each category.

To properly determine the probability factor for any potential order, therefore, multiply the possibility of your company's chances of being selected by the possibility the customer will spend the money and buy from anyone.

Here's my proven order forecasting method. Four columns: 1. Purchase Probability Percent. (What is the likelihood that they will spend the money with anybody and make a purchase). 2. Your Company's Probability Percent (Your company's chance of winning if they spend the money) 3. Factored Probability Percent. (Column 1 times column 2 – the likelihood of you getting the order. 4. Factored $. (Column 4 times the size of the forecasted order).

Purchase Probability %	Your Company's Probability %	Factored Probability %	Factored $
25% Early 50% Maybe 75% Budgeted 90% Committed	25% Early 50% Competitive 75% Winning 90% Want you	Multiply the Purchase % times Your Company's Probability %	Factored % times Order $
Likelihood the prospect will spend money on a product like yours	*Prospect's feelings about you*	*Your chances getting an order from this prospect*	*$ amount for forecasting purposes*

Overly optimistic sales forecasts

Many so-called "lost" sales do not go to the competition. Instead the customer delays or cancels the procurement. This factor is often overlooked by inexperienced forecasters.

For example, let's say there's a 75 percent probability your prospect is going to spend $10,000 for a product like the one you are selling. (Note: This factor has nothing to do with your product or company's chances; it's simply predicting the likelihood the prospect will spend that kind of money with someone in the expected time frame.)

Let's also say that your prospect told you he favors your product and company and will likely choose you as the vendor. In other words, there is about a 75 percent chance you will be selected.

What, then, is the probability you will make the sale? The answer is not 75 percent. Instead the probability you will get the order is the product of 75 percent (they will spend money) times 75 percent (they'll select your company/product) or 56 percent. That's right, instead of winning in 3 out of 4 situations like this, your chances are closer to 2 out of 4!

Wrap Up

It's almost impossible to make money if you don't know how much money will be coming in. Without a reasonable revenue/collection forecast, you're going to struggle trying to figure out how much you can afford to spend. Predictability begets profitability.

Chapter 32: Post Sales

Keep your customers happy.

What will make your customers feel good about having chosen to do business with you? This will not be easy if your salesperson has oversold the customer. Train your salespeople to know when to stop selling and start negotiating. Give yourself an opportunity to over deliver. Promise less, deliver more. Your aims are:

- **Customer loyalty.** Personal service is the best way to create a loyal customer. Spend quality time with your customers. Look for problems. Nothing beats personal attention. What can you do to make the customer feel loyal to you?
- **Follow on sales.** The best time to make a repeat sale is immediately after the customer has bought something—while in a buying mood. Consider sending a letter acknowledging each order within 24 hours after purchase. Offer the buyer a great deal on an additional product or service received with the initial purchase.
- **Customer Database.** Make sure you capture the name, title, address, and telephone number of every customer.
- **Existing customers are your best prospects.** How long will you wait before you contact this customer again? Who will make contact and how? How can you make sure the contact happens? Who will be responsible?

Customer Service

A classic ad agency saying goes like this: "Creative wins 'em. Customer service loses 'em."

This holds true for almost any industry or business. Quality customer service can make up for a lot of other flaws. Do it right and your first-time customers will become perpetual customers. Technology can be of great assistance here and can make the difference between mediocre and extraordinary customer service. For example, Customer Relationship Management (CRM) software and online databases regularly remind your service representatives to spend more time on customer service.

Software and technology are evolving all the time. Use it. Field service representatives (and customers) can gather support information at the click of a mouse. Companies can also use this information to provide additional services for their customers. For example, informing mobile customers they are nearing their data plan limits and not to worry because their limits have been automatically extended at no charge.

Training

Properly designed customer service training programs are highly interactive. They focus on what's important and what it takes to get the job done. When service people discover that these programs don't waste their time, they learn quickly and enthusiastically. This form of training is private, fast, and self-paced. Slow learners can review and take time for extra practice; fast learners can skip over what they already know. It also saves money since there are no expensive classrooms, unpredictable instructors, or travel and lodging costs. Further, service people spend less time away from the job and they don't have to wait for a scheduled class.

Product knowledge databases

Online product knowledge databases make information available 24/7. They can keep your service people trained and up to date.

All the service representative must do is access the database from a smartphone or personal computer. There they can find the latest installation instructions, answers to common questions, operating instructions, part numbers, prerequisites, configurations, pricing, interchangeable parts, and so on.

Inaccurate information is the most common cause of mistakes and errors. An online database will instantly reduce the occurrence of both. You'll soon wonder how you ever did without it.

Lastly, an online database makes everyone more accountable. Total visibility and tracking mean nothing falls through the cracks. Quantitative data is instantly available on how long callers wait, how long it takes to resolve problems, and how many service calls are made per day.

Response time

Compress the time it takes to respond to customer requests. By helping service people identify problems, test, isolate trouble, troubleshoot, and replace parts, product-knowledge databases reduce errors and shorten customer response time. They also promote teamwork since customer service teams can share information and interact without having to be in the same room at the same time. Anyone can post technical issues and solutions for general use. A creative solution posted by one person can benefit everyone immediately.

Use of automation

Automate your customer services representative's labor-intensive work. Document imaging hardware lets you scan incoming correspondence directly into customer files and eliminates time-consuming data entry. An online document library can serve as a repository for customer service forms, letters, and other customer service documents. Customer service representatives can bring up the original customer paperwork. Guesswork is eliminated. Customers feel good about doing business with a vendor whose representatives know all about them and their situation. They should never feel like strangers.

Service people can now spend more time on customer service and less on paperwork. In short, they can provide higher quality services to more customers in less time.

Wrap Up

- Take the time to know your customers. Turn your customers into friends, or at least people who see you as friendly.
- Stay in touch. What are their interests other than business?
- Fast and efficient customer service solutions to customer problems are superior ways to turn first-time customers into perpetual ones.

TECHNOLOGY

Chapter 33: Technology

Being tech savvy is not optional. The Internet is the most powerful marketing weapon in history. The COVID-19 pandemic made the Internet—with its connectivity, retention, and reach—a vital component in just about all business dealings.

The power of the Internet is not just its ability to reach wide audiences, but also in the collective voice and power of its users. It's a two-way highway that collects user inputs, opinions, ratings, and comments; aggregates the statistics; and displays the results back to the very audience that generated them. Meanwhile, the world's digital infrastructure is in a constant state of flux.

And as time has moved on, the Internet has become a one-screen world and mobile phones have become the screen of choice for interpersonal communications, news gathering, entertainment and shopping.

By no means do the following paragraphs tell you everything you need to know about using technology to elevate the profile of your company and trigger sales. They are designed to point you toward key topics you need to plunge into, learn about, and determine how to apply the information to your business.

Website

Your Internet presence is still rooted at your own web address. Your website and your multi-billion-dollar competitor's site sit side-by-side inviting comparison. The Internet gives you the opportunity to compete with giants on a playing field that's reasonably level and certainly affordable. In short, your website must be easy to find and competitive; that is, appealing, engaging, relevant, and reflective of your company's culture and style.

There is also no escaping that just about everyone, when they first hear about your company, will look you up on the Internet. It's a way to determine your legitimacy and it's also your one chance to make a first impression. Visitors who find you start by entering your company name, or something related to what you do, into one of the search engines, and will expect your website address to appear prominently in the list of sites the engine returns.

Your website has two audiences: your visitors, the people you want to do business with and the search engines, so they can direct first-time visitors right to your front door most effectively. As online, virtual communications have become commonplace, provide your web visitors with a link enabling them to book a virtual meeting with you.

Once new visitors arrive, you have precious little time to show them what you do and what makes you different. The best sites use quality images, with just a few, short easy-to-read paragraphs on each page. Menu tabs are meant to navigate and direct users to deeper content so they should mean what they say. Downloads and videos should run quickly. And, again, you must have the right information for search engines.

Expectations

Before you embark on a website development project, be clear about your goals and objectives. Your website should reflect who you are, what you're selling, what makes you different, and why you're the best choice.

Using the competition

How well does your website compete? Prospective customers will view your competitors' sites and comparison-shop at the same time they visit yours.

You need to know what you're up against.

Begin your Internet competitor search right in your own backyard.

Step 1. Use very specific keywords (for example, plumbers in Sterling, Virginia). Record your findings.

Step 2. Widen your search (for example, plumbers in Virginia). Again, record your findings.

Step 3. Now do a broader search (for example, plumbers).

Looking at competitors' sites from beyond your geographic region may not seem to make sense, that is, most people will call a local plumber to fix a pipe, not someone outside the area. But what you are doing is looking for new ideas. By expanding your search, you will broaden your view, see how others are presenting themselves, and likely discover approaches you would never have considered.

Once you've done a little research, you should be ready to move ahead and start creating or upgrading your site. Keep in mind that this truly is the age of skepticism and everybody suffers from sensory overload. Any claim you make without relevance or proof is useless. Remember that you only have a few seconds to make the point. Think headline and visual. Get right to the point and state clearly your offer.

Basic design

At a minimum you need the following pages:

Home, where most of your visitors start to review your site. Get them interested quickly. Your objective is to get them to go more deeply into your site._

About You

Products/Services

Contact Us

You may also want to have a section devoted to Blogs and Recent Events, where you post news releases.

Budget

How much can you afford to spend? Whatever you decide, give yourself at least a 20 -25 percent buffer on the development side. For example, if you can afford $5,000, commit $4,000. Use that extra $1,000 to cover the additional features or embellishments that you forgot and decide you need once the site is up and running.

Building a website is akin to building a home. Choose your subcontractors carefully and budget reasonably. It is also an ongoing process. On your first pass, include all the necessities and only those luxuries you can afford now and that won't take very long to implement. You can always add features later—and you always will. Stick to the basics in the beginning; your initial priorities are to get it up and running promptly and operating flawlessly.

Recurring (Monthly Expenses)
Site maintenance and upgrades
Search engine optimization
Pay-per-click advertising
Hosting
URL renewals

Non-recurring Expenses
Site development
Visuals/photography
Copywriting

Time

Your development timeframe, whether you build it in-house or use an outside web firm, depends on the complexity of your website. And of course, how much money you're willing to spend. For a small, simple website, it is reasonable to expect development to take four to six weeks—assuming you already have all your content together. Again, concentrate on functionality.

Have your designer create a graphic prototype (mock-up) early on so you can see what it's going to look like. Show it to a few people and get their reactions. This way, you can have the designer make the big changes quickly—before you've spent a lot of money on something you're not going to use. Once you launch the site, you'll be making more changes, but you'll have something you feel good about right from the beginning.

Style

Style is the general look of the site—layout, colors, fonts, and graphics. Certain websites (like one representing an architecture firm) lend themselves more to an artistic style, while others (like an electrician's) do not.

Assume you are shopping on the web and find what you were looking for at two different sites. One site is stripped down, text-heavy, and has little regard for style; the other is clearly laid out and uses headlines, text, and images effectively. Chances are you will favor and trust the firm with the better-looking site.

Your website should be different than any other and offer visitors a unique experience. However, this doesn't mean you can't take inspiration from other sites. If you like certain aspects of a competitor's site, come up with a variant that retains what you liked, but has your own look and feel. If you simply mimic your competitor's website (rather than improving on it), you'll have nothing that sets you apart and you may also face legal infringement issues.

Pay special attention to more established websites because web content normally evolves through expensive trial and error. If the competitor has been online for a long period of time, what has survived probably works.

Navigation

Visitors want to find what they are looking for quickly. On a web site it's called the Navigation Bar: simple menus, buttons, informative banners, and other graphic elements that keep your visitors from getting lost and help them move around.

The navigation bar is an integral part of the design. It should have clearly placed and labeled links to guide your visitors. Button placement should be consistent on every page.

Testing your navigation system can be problematic because by the time you realize it needs fixing, the site is usually up and open to the public. One technique you can use is what we call the Take 3 Principle—where you progressively test your scheme.

Take 1. Select a savvy Internet user, someone who is an expert when it comes to site navigation and using/searching the Internet.

Take 2. Select an average website user.

Take 3. Finally, select the most inexperienced and amateur web user you can find.

Ask all three testers to navigate your site on a general basis, and then have each look for something (e.g., a certain product or service). Sit behind them, but don't say anything, and observe how they click through your site. Once they have finished, get their comments, and make the necessary changes before launching.

Content

Web content is often rushed and poorly executed. Do not just upload some copy from your brochure or your latest PowerPoint presentation. Instead, condense your messages into short paragraphs with clearly labeled subheads. Look back at your competitors' sites and see what they had to say. Use keywords and keyword phrases that prospective visitors might use on a search engine to see what you have to say.

Your message must be clear, concise, informative, and easy to read. Most people spend less than four seconds on a page before moving on. If you are not a skilled writer, find someone on your staff that is or hire a professional.

Never use content that does not belong to you. This is a clear violation of copyright laws and is something that can easily be caught. Besides, your company is original; your message should be as well.

Video and/or audio

Take advantage of the medium and appeal to more than one sense. Try replacing ordinary text with a video demonstration—a presentation with a voice-over or an animated flash-piece. Provide enough information for new prospects to qualify themselves. Videos are great for this and they're also great for YouTube exposure.

Be careful, though, not to overload your site. A recent Harris poll revealed that over 40 percent of adults abandon a website or their online shopping carts when they either get confused or encounter a problem with a vendor's website.

In summary, start off with a simple approach that works intuitively. Save the fancy stuff for later. Invite a stranger or two to comment and execute your "call to action" like buying something or filling out a form and making a submission—all before going live. Restaurants often have soft openings, where they don't advertise but, instead, open silently and work out the wrinkles. That's good advice for your new website.

Social Networks

Once your website works the way you want it to, you need to turn your attention to the Internet's social networks. These enable users to share experiences, share facts about themselves, maintain online relationships, and share knowledge.

Something simple but powerful happens when people share knowledge. Word-of-mouth, especially dissatisfaction, can spread exponentially and go viral quickly. Companies cannot control this, so they have learned to thrive on it. Social networks like Facebook, Twitter, LinkedIn, and others have become fascinating to businesses. Just imagine a rich and ripe pool of customers, whom you can pick out of the crowd based on the demographics they provide about themselves. Or better, imagine a whole host of statistics at your fingertips that let you understand these peoples' purchasing habits, preferences, and what's on their wish lists.

Social Media

The earliest forms of social media evolved from the simplest "talk" commands on Unix/Linux computer platforms. By knowing login information, users could query the system to see which parties were logged on. Primitive as it was, that communication could take place in real time across buildings and was well beyond what email could do.

Soon after that AOL entered the scene and nearly everyone in college joined AOL Instant Messenger or AIM. The login or "name" chosen by a user could be shared so that a multi-user conversation was possible across networks, college campuses, and cities. No longer was information isolated to an event or a locale. If it were happening somewhere, the word spread fast and couldn't be retracted.

Late 90s

Cell phones hadn't come into play among the general population, although many businesspeople relied on large versions reminiscent of the spy's "shoe phone" on the TV program *Get Smart*.

The late 90s brought broader-bandwidth ISDN and DSL into telecom, which made phone-line channels available for data in addition to voice. Even with plain old telephone service (POTS), this data bandwidth was available, but was used by select few for administrative purposes or by doctors carrying pagers.

With ISDN and DSL bandwidth, phones soon introduced new capabilities focused on data versus voice. Texting had begun although most people still preferred to make a phone call as texting was considered rude. As people got busier, phones with their dedicated focus became more burdensome versus the ability to multi-task. People began to see that with social media, multiple conversations could be held at once without requiring dedicated focus.

Social media as norm

People started using their phones less for talking and much more for everything else. Apps became a "thing." Early app developers took mundane ideas and capitalized on them and became millionaires virtually overnight. Blackberry was instrumental in launching the "app" age because their platform included many such functional tools. However, Blackberry could not keep up with the demand to create different apps. Google did realize this potential and created an open source platform, allowing developers of all ages and skills levels to be inventive and creative and to launch their applications into the wild blue yonder. Developers thrived on popularity alone as apps spread by word of mouth.

The monetization angle came much later as advertisers realized the money that could be made from people simply using the apps. They began to pay developers for advertising within their apps. While individual payouts were miniscule, they added up with millions of views. Spam was born and will be here to stay. Users growing tired of advertising began to look for ways to avoid ads and the subscription economy was born so that users could opt to pay a small monthly fee to avoid advertisements. The rise of homegrown apps on open source platforms also created opportunity for bad actors to take advantage of un-savvy tech users. Malicious software (malware) also spread virally just as news and jokes did from user to user.

A world-wide phenomenon

The free-for-all was quieted and brought under control to some extent by Apple, with its slick new iPhone and iMac/iPod/iPad line of products that brought design appeal to technology for the lay user. Mobile phones flourished globally even more so than in the US, where lobbies worked to keep legacy systems in play because of the investment made in infrastructure like ground and land lines. Europe and Asia weren't burdened with infrastructure and with a hungry populous, decided to skip making deep land line investments and opted instead for cheaper cell tower connectivity. By continually lowering mobile phones costs and advancing apps and bandwidth, the telecom industry helped to create the modern era of web technology, apps, Internet of Things (IOT) and connected systems.

Pros and cons of mass communications

Social Media was inevitably the outcome and remains a wild, wild west of communication. Big industries have had to bow to the consumer when negative viral news spread about a company and little guys became big overnight by virtue of their viral popularity. The internet became a great equalizer as well as a star maker and a limelight destroyer for many. Today social media is a dodgy arena for individuals and corporations because of the risk to personal reputation.

Social Media and Marketing

Social Media has helped marketing evolve into a two-way dialogue. When using social media for marketing it becomes an online conversation. Don't pitch, instead befriend.

Having online conversations can be good and bad. The old line about having one unhappy customer tell five or ten is no longer valid; now with social media that number can be hundreds or thousands. So, take care. Social media enables you to connect with your customers and prospects while shaping their perception of you and your products.

Working all the social media sites takes time. If you don't have that kind of time, go all in on one social platform and make your mark there.

Proper, effective uses

Use social media to:

- Increase traffic to your website by placing a link to your web site on your social media.
- That link can also help improve your search engine results.
- Use Facebook's Get Notifications to keep an eye on your competition
- Blogging lets you brand yourself as an expert in your field
- Uncover new prospects

Social Media	Audience. What it is.	What's it for
Blogs (Bloggers) Platforms include: blogger.com, wordpress.org	Like an online Op Ed column where people can read, subscribe, or supply commentary for others to read. Blogs are the content engines driving the social web and are critical to any digital marketing initiative. Blogs contribute to SEO and PR opportunities. Make your blog titles include the right keywords.	Many companies provide blogs like testimonials about their products or services. The air of authenticity (i.e., an unsolicited opinion) is inviting to users. Some professional bloggers make a living this way because they build a fan following that attracts advertisers. Google likes How To and Why articles. Can be an online diary and/or for sharing online discoveries.

Tweets (Twitter) www.twitter.com	These are blogs limited to 140 characters. Some call them micro-blogs. Broadcast your perceptions, new ideas and reactions. Where you go to meet people.	Anyone can tweet about anything. Many celebrities and politicians have built subscriber bases for their tweets. You can do the same to keep your customers feeling special.
API Application Programming Interface	An instruction manual of sorts that lets technical users develop customized applets or mini programs on a specific platform.	Create a mini application that entices users to interact and lets you gather statistics and build a following. For example, non-profits are finding creative uses to further their causes.
Facebook www.facebook.com	Social network for everyone, world-wide. Where you go to talk to and interact with people you already know. Embed your Facebook review on your website.	Facebook is a platform for friends to share pictures, opinions, and passions, and to promote friendships and connections. A presence here can put you in touch with thousands of people and their closest friends
LinkedIn www.linkedIn.com	Social network for professionals If your target is business-to-business, then having a professional LinkedIn presence is a must. Market your business, yourself, and your abilities.	LinkedIn is fast becoming the place to find candidates for jobs and for job postings that are referrals from friends. It's so much more personal than Monster.com!

Instagram	Use it to capture, edit & share photos, videos & messages with friends & family.	Owned by Facebook. Account posts can be shared publicly or with pre-approved followers.

Crowd Funding

Crowd funding platforms provide entrepreneurs and businesses with a means to raise capital. Some compensate their contributors with a reward, some in the form of debt payback or with stock in their company.

Reward: Two of the more popular sites are Indiegogo and Kickstarter. Here donors are rewarded with products or mementos.

Debt: SoMoLend and Endurance Lending Network are web-based lending platforms for obtaining debt capital.

Equity Investment: AngelList and others provide businesses with capital in return for shares of stock for participating investors.

Cloud Computing

With cloud computing, an organization's internally hosted servers and applications are shifted to remotely based servers' locations and accessed by the Internet.

Aside from the fact that hardware and software maintenance and upkeep become someone else's responsibility, Cloud computing services can also be paid for on an "as used" basis. For example, services and software are often billed just like you're charged for electricity, that is, you only pay for what you use.

By now most of the world's largest companies are storing customer-sensitive data in the public cloud. Because cloud computing purchase massive amounts of hardware and power and their charges can be variable rather than fixed costs, pricing to users has becoming much more attractive.

Marketing Automation

This is primarily used by marketing departments to automate communications and marketing programs. It measures marketing ROI, automates repetitive tasks, and facilitates email marketing, social posting, and marketing on multiple online channels. Helps to better align marketing and sales.

Find some technical help. You'll have to figure out what role the Web will play in your business plan. Certainly, you'll need a website, visitors, and some presence in the networking arenas. Concentrate on who you are targeting, what you are saying (or demonstrating), and making sure the search engines know all about you.

The first step is to find a professional web site development firm and, while you're at it, find a company that knows all about search engine marketing. Make them prove to you they can make a difference.

Wrap Up

Be assured your competition is going to exploit technology. You need to do the same. You have no choice. Find someone to help you do this. Getting popular is worth every penny.

At a minimum, in addition to your website exploit the advantages of social media with a blog, a Facebook, Twitter and LinkedIn presence. If you don't think you can do justice to all four, do just one and make it extraordinary.

Chapter 34: Search Engine Marketing

Once upon a time selling over the Internet was as simple as putting up a site: "Build it and they will come." Today, that sounds naïve and stupid. Knowing where (and how) your target customers shop online is the first step to effectively selling over the Internet.

Most people use the major search engines to find what they want. Search engine marketing usually refers to using paid advertisements that appear on search result pages. Typically, these ads are purchased via a "pay-per-click" (PPC) model meaning you pay each time a user clicks on your ads. You'll need exposure on Google and Bing. Google Ads is by far the most popular.

Organic search engine results vs PPC results

There are primarily two ways to achieve exposure on the search engines: organically and via pay-per-click (PPC) advertising. Organic search results cannot be bought. When search engines rank websites organically for keywords, they rely on hundreds of different attributes based on their ever-changing algorithm. One of the most critical attributes to attain valuable organic exposure is high quality and compelling content. See the next chapter on Search Engine Optimization (SEO).

Pay-Per-Click (PPC) campaigns provide you with quick, predictable, and targeted traffic. Properly set-up and managed, they are an important part of any search engine marketing strategy.

PPC marketing allows you to bid on as many keywords as you want without changing anything on your site. Whenever a keyword is searched, your ad will be displayed. However, since you're paying per click, it's critical you match the searchers intent with your ad copy and the landing page message. For as much as search engines love and reward high levels of engagement, they equally hate high levels of bounces and abandoned sites.

The amount you pay per click depends primarily on the popularity of the keyword. The more popular the keyword, the more advertisers are willing to pay. Keyword groups, comprised of targeted keyword phrases, will not only attract more qualified visitors, but have a lower cost-per-click (CPC). Targeted groups will lead to higher engagement. The search engines will reward you for this with lower costs per click and higher placement.

Search Patterns

You need to ascertain how your target buyers search the Web. Different people use different keywords, even when searching for the same product. Normally, the longer the keyword phrase, the more targeted the search. Someone who knows exactly what he or she wants will be specific. For example, a search for "flowers" doesn't indicate the searcher wants to buy flowers; a search for "buy flowers" does. A phrase like "buy flowers in Long Island NY" reveals even more.

What are the obvious one-word keywords and keyword phrases (two or three words) people will use to find your product or service?

Competitive search strategies

Prior to performing in-depth keyword research, go to a search engine and type in some obvious keywords. Results will reveal how your competitors react to these queries. Repeat this process with a variety of related keywords. If you sell books, for example, search keywords/phrases such as "book sellers," "book vendor," "purchase books," "buy book online," and so on. Do this on all the major search engines (Google, Bing, DuckDuckGo, etc..). The purpose of this exercise is to get a high-level understanding of the competitive search landscape.

Which keywords or phrases are most popular, that is, bring up the most competitors?
Which competitors ads rank highest for each keyword/phrase?
What could you do to differentiate and stick out via ad text and/or offering?

Now is the time to start thinking about what you can do to 1) give the search engines reasons for ranking your site higher within the paid ads section (aka sponsored listings) of the results page. The best way to do this is to make compelling ads that are specific to the intent of the search query. Having a variety of ads targeting niche keywords will increase your click through rates (CTRs) which Google rewards since they want their searchers to be satisfied with the results they've been presented. The better your ad matches the intent of the searchers and the higher engagement rate achieved, the greater the likelihood of getting a boost in placement for your ads and 2) provide the searcher with a right-to-the-point landing page, for example, a special page or section designed especially for that query's intent. Again, search engines reward engagement and the better your ad and landing experience satisfy the searcher intent the better.

Keywords

What keywords can you use that will attract the most and best new customers? Coming up with unique keywords that have not been targeted by your competition can give you a big advantage, especially in more competitive industries.

Segment your customers into related search groups. Then further segment them into niche keyword groups. This will enable you to cost-effectively speak directly to customers in each segment.

For example, if you sell tennis shoes, running shoes, and basketball shoes, segment their keywords into those three different niche groups.

Different keyword phrases suggest different responses depending on the consumer's needs. According to Google's search gurus, Consumer Need States predict intent.

Consumer Need States	
Surprise Me	Educate Me
Help Me	Impress Me
Reassure Me	Thrill Me

For example, "What car should I buy if I make $150,000 a year?" sounds like an "Impress Me" need. Or a "What car should I buy that would make me different from all my business colleagues?" sounds like a "Surprise Me" need. By paying attention to people's needs, you have a much better chance of influencing their decision and making a sale.

Landing pages

These are the lead capture pages you use when someone clicks on your search engine listing. These page's content needs to be specific to the searched keyword and intent of searcher. A squeeze page is a landing page created to solicit opt-in email addresses and other contact information. What works here is a free something such as a White Paper or eBook—kind of an ethical bribe.

Beginning your Pay-Per-Click campaign

Google and Bing each have their own PPC platforms: Google Ads and Microsoft Advertising (formerly Bing Ads). Google has the most potential traffic so many businesses advertise first with Google. When you see certain keywords and ads performing well on Google, consider taking the highest performing keywords/ads and start a Bing campaign with what has the best likelihood of success. Focus on the quality, not the quantity, of visitors.

PPC Keyword Selection

Keywords are at the heart of your campaign. Since you are paying per click, you want niche and targeted keyword phrases. As noted previously, single keywords can have their place in a campaign, but keyword phrases almost always attract a more qualified visitor. In fact, keyword phrases will typically cost a fraction of the cost per click than a broad single word keyword. To begin creating keyword lists, use some of the keyword research tools like wordtracker.com, ahrefs.com, Google's Keyword Tool, and Microsoft Advertising's Keyword Planner Tool.

You can also set your PPC campaign not to trigger ads when certain keywords are searched (called negative keywords). For example, people searching on the word "free" normally aren't in a buying mood, so "free" is a common negative keyword.

Ad Creation

Ads that display your keyword phrases must be compelling enough to stand out from the crowd. They must entice the right people and turn away the wrong (unqualified) people before they click on your ad. So, don't generalize but be very specific in your PPC ad copy. Constantly test multiple ads that target the same keyword sets. Having at least two to three ads running at once will give you constant data that allows you to pause what isn't working and create variations of what is working.

Ad Groups

You can respond to related searches with the same targeted ads if you group similar keyword phrases. For example, the keyword phrases "buy flowerpots," "pots for flowers," and "flowerpots for sale" can all trigger the same type ads. It's common for advertisers to have ten, twenty or (many) more ad groups in a PPC campaign. Again, it's critical you have a specific landing page to match that searchers intent.

Conversion Tracking

It's very important to track which keywords and ads work best. Which keywords and ads result in a sale, a lead, a visit, or a phone call. Conversion tracking is critical to get the best bang for your marketing buck. Conversion tracking also allows you to use many automated optimized bidding settings available within the PPC platforms.

Online Advertising Venues

Google Ads (formerly Adwords). Since Google is the master of search engine marketing, its advertising platform Google Ads is the biggest platform for PPC marketing. Google Ads lets you create text, image or video-based advertisements targeting people who search for specific keywords or show interest in particular topics.

Its search ads have made the buyer-seeks-seller strategy (aka inbound marketing) the method of choice amongst all sellers regardless of size, industry, or target market. The main Google Ads options include:

- **Search Ads**—You target specific keywords people are typing in as they search. Advertisers compete in an online auction with competitors for top placements.
- **Display Network**—You can place text, image, and video ads across all of Google's display network. These sites reach over 90 percent of Internet users worldwide. (Source: Comscore).
- **Remarketing**—After someone has been to your website, you can follow that individual with specific ads as that person surfs the internet.

Microsoft Advertising (formerly Bing Ads). Like Google Ads, Bing has search ads, a display network and remarketing. The Bing search engine has a much smaller audience than Google, which normally makes bidding on keywords less expensive.

Facebook. Facebook ads are primarily offered as pay-per-click or CPM (cost per 1000 ad impressions). Facebook lets you target by creating targeted audience lists. You can create different audience lists that take into consideration various demographic makeups and user interests.

You Tube. You Tube also works on a pay-per-click or CPM basis. Here, you only pay for the viewing when someone watches your video for a predetermined amount of time or of course if they click on the ad. You can advertise on You Tube utilizing the Google Ads user interface.

LinkedIn. LinkedIn also offers pay-per-click or CPM bidding. For many businesses LinkedIn is the most effective social network at reaching a target market, especially for B2B.

Wrap Up

The right keyword phrases are crucial for a successful PPC campaign. Having a high level of engagement is critical to keeping your visitors happy as well as the search engines. PPC is the fastest way to make something happen and you're in control.

Chapter 35: Search Engine Optimization (SEO)

Unlike PPC, you don't pay the search engines to achieve a high ad placement. Your position occurs as the result of keyword searches and how best your website/pages satisfy those queries. Search positions can vary as search engine algorithms change regularly, typically at least once per month. Therefore, SEO is not a strategy in which you apply once and forget—especially not in competitive markets.

Search engine optimization comes in different degrees. These extend from the essentials (for example, high quality content, unique title tags, and compelling description tags) to more time-consuming and advanced considerations (like quality link acquisition, internal navigation/link structure, site load time, and core keyword and topical keyword mentions).

A methodical SEO approach is the best way to optimize your site for search engines. Take one step at a time, do the most important first. Here are seven essential steps for SEO.

SEO Essential #1—Title tag

This is the link on the search results page that connects the viewer to your site. On your web page, the title tag appears above your browser's address bar. The title tag serves primarily two purposes. It provides keywords that help search engines better rank the site. It also helps your listing to achieve more searcher engagement when the content of the title tag is compelling.

Improve your organic ranking by using important keywords in your title tags while providing a compelling message to encourage a searcher to click your listing.

To view a page's Title tag, right click the page and click on "view source" to see what the source code looks like. You should see the title tag toward the top of the code. It will look like this: <title> Title is Here</title>.

Title tag check points
Are important keywords used (but not overused) in the title tag of each page?
Are title tags concise (about 50-60 characters)?
Does each page have a unique title tag that gives an accurate description of that page?
Does each page's title tag encourage a searcher to click your listing?
Do keywords in each title tag also appear in that page's body text?
Is there only one title tag per page?

SEO Essential #2—Meta Description tags

Although meta description tags aren't usually part of the search algorithms, a well written description tag can help increase Click Through Rates (CTRs) and engagement, which Google does use for rankings. Description tags are the short body of text that appear under the title tag within the search results. The description tag can be found toward the top of the page in the source code.

Description Meta tag: <meta name="description" content="-Description goes here">

Meta Description tag check points
Does each page have a unique description tag?
Is your description tag compelling and encouraging searchers to click your listing as opposed to a competitor?

Is the description tag to the point and giving an accurate expectation of what your page is about?
Are the page's targeted keywords tactfully used in the description tag?
Do you have only one description tag per page?
Are description tags concise (about 50 to 160 characters)

SEO Essential #3—Body Text

The main text of a webpage is called body text (aka body copy). Always write for the visitor and not necessarily for the search engines. You want to keep your visitors engaged, and never come across as spammy. With that said, tactfully adding specific keywords is suggested, but also using related topical keywords is important. For example, if you're targeting "lawyers" you should also include terms like attorney, law firm, legal, and so on. One note here is that although search engines (especially Google) are getting much better at reading text in images and flash, not all can do so. Therefore, it's important to use HTML as the main form of text on your web pages.

Body text check points
Is the body text unique (not duplicated on other sites/pages) and high quality?
Does the body text mention important keywords and topical terms?
Is there over-repetition of any one keyword?
Does the most important keyword(s) within the body text also appear in the title and description tags?
Does your website use primarily HTML body text?

SEO Essential #4—No broken links

Both the search engines and your visitors use your site's hyperlinks to move from one page to another. Broken links prevent search engines from accessing your subpages and visitors from staying on your site.

SEO Essential #5—Link text

Link text (aka anchor text) are the words clicked on that takes your visitors to another webpage or website. Using keywords and relevant topics within the link text (as opposed to "click here") gives visitors and the search engines more information about the content and nature of the linked web page/site. Although keywords and topics within link text is important, it's even more important to ensure the links appear natural and not keyword stuffed or spammy. Link text should be relevant to the page being linked to. Only link to useful pages/sites that are adding value to your visitors and web page.

Link text check points
Is there non-optimized link text (for example, "click here")? If so, where can I change the generic link text to something more descriptive?
Does the link text within your pages appear natural and not spammy?
Are links adding to the user experience? If they are not adding value, remove the links.

SEO Essential #6—Site Speed

A website that loads fast is critical to a happy visitor. No one wants to wait seconds for a page to load. There are just too many options and people will leave a slow site and go to a quicker one. In addition, site speed is one of the most important search engine ranking attributes. Faster sites get more favorable rankings and better visitor engagement than slower sites.

SEO Essential #7—No dead pages

Dead pages are just that—dead and not accessible. That's because the page has been removed, deleted, or the URL was changed. When this occurs, the browser will inform the viewer the "page does not exist." (also known as a 404 error). Check your links to make sure all your pages are live. Dead pages are dead ends for visitors and the search engines. Don't just delete or remove a page, rather redirect it to a live page that is most similar in topic to the page you're redirecting. Tools like screamingfrog.co.uk/ can crawl your site and help you detect dead pages.

Dead pages check points
Are all the links in my website leading to live pages?
Are all old (no longer needed) pages redirected to a relevant live page?
Have you checked your entire website for dead links? Use site crawler tools to expedite the effort.

Additional search engine considerations include:

Link Popularity. When search engines rank websites, they need to separate legitimate sites from ephemeral or flash-in-the-pan sites. One way they do this is by considering the quality and quantity of links leading to your website. When high-quality websites link to your website, the search engines use that as an indicator that the site has been up and running for some period and is serious and important.

Sitemap Creation. There are two types of sitemaps. One is a visible page on your website. It lists all your site pages and has links to each. This type of sitemap can be valuable to both visitors and the search engines. The second sitemap is behind the scenes and only used by the search engines to help them know which pages to include in the search results. This type of sitemap is typically an XML (Extensible Markup Language) file. Using an automated sitemap generator (for example, xml-sitemaps.com) is the best way to quickly create a sitemap.

Page (File) Names. Webpage file names can add keyword relevance to web pages for both visitors and search engines. For example, a flower shop may have a subpage on its site named page4.htm that is focused on roses. This page should be renamed to roses.htm, red-roses.htm, or any name containing a relevant keyword/phrase.

Headline Tags. Search engines read these, so use keywords in your headline tags. These are normally found just above a block of text and allow you to specify print size (from <H1> </H1>, the largest, to <H6> </H6>, the smallest) of your headline. The <H1> </H1> tag should be used only once on a given page. Other size tags can be used multiple times. Each headline tags should reinforce the copy of the page.

Search engine no-noes are:

- **Mirrored Sites.** A mirrored site is one with the same content as another site at a different web address. Search engines do not like mirrored web sites and may refuse to index such websites. That's because search engines want to provide searchers with a variety of results. When the same content comes from multiple sites, searchers are getting fewer choices and may be unable to find what they are really seeking. Closely related is duplicate content. This is content that is the same on different websites or on the same website. This too must be avoided.
- **Repetitive Keywords.** No matter what part of your website you are optimizing (title tags, body text, headlines, etc..), do not continually repeat the same keywords phrases. This is a tactic, called keyword stuffing, that spammers use to get their spam sites ranked. Search engines don't like it and viewers will find it difficult to read stuffed text. Write the text for your readers and use keyword phrases naturally.
- **Hidden Text.** Super-small text (invisible to the eye) or text the same color as the page background is called hidden or invisible text. Hidden text is considered spam by the search engines and any site that uses it can expect to be penalized or even banned by the search engines.

Wrap Up

There are many attributes the search engines consider when ranking websites in the organic (non-paid) search results. Focus on high quality content that engages your visitors. Make sure you use important keywords where applicable. Take care of the technical components of your site like site speed, XML sitemaps, and making sure all links and pages are live and not "dead."

Chapter 36: Google Analytics

This free powerful tool provides you with a comprehensive way to collect visitor and usage statistics. You, as a website owner, must use it. Without it, you will not know what's happening on your website. With it, you'll get all the information you could ever imagine. Take the time to learn how to access these metrics. They are more than fascinating and can help you turn an ordinary website into a sales and marketing machine.

Go to https://marketingplatform.google.com/about/analytics and create a Google account. Then have your website administrator add the Analytics tracking code (script) to the relevant pages of your website and set you up with an account and analytic reports. When you first log into Analytics it will be somewhat dauting. Don't fret. Soon you'll know more about your website activity and online marketing than you ever imagined. Analytics can literally tell you everything you ever imaged about how your web site is behaving. Analytics has four major sections

- **Audience.** Measures traffic into your website.

  Overview. Top level view.

  Demographics. Age and gender of your audience.

  Interests. Users by affinity and marketing categories

  Geo. Languages and locations of your audience

  Behavior. Comparisons of new and returning visitors.

Technology. Your visitors' browsers, operating systems, and networks.

Mobile. Devices being used to access your web site.

Custom. Reports you define

Users Flow. A visualization on how your visitors move through you site

- **Acquisitions.** Where your visitors come from.

  Overview. Top channels sending visitors to your website

  All traffic. Analyze where most of your traffic comes from

  Google Ads. Details on how your advertisements are working

  Search Console. Landing page and website performance

  Social. Which sites are feeding you visitors and producing conversions?

  Campaigns. Keywords. Cost analysis

- **Behavior.** How they move thru your site. What pages are most popular?

  Overview. Number of page views. Avg. time on page. Bounce rates

  Behavior Flow. Paths visitors take from first page to last page

  Site Content. How visitors engage with pages on your site

  Site Speed. Identifies pages of your site that may need load time optimization

  Site Search. Metrics for visitors who use your web site's search box

  Events. Track specific interactions on your site like clicks on external links

Google Ads. Measure Google Paid Search performance

Experiments. Helps you conduct simple A/B testing, for example, landing page variations

- **Conversions.** Tracks website conversions.

  Goals. Which web pages are converting?

  Ecommerce. Conversion rates, transactions, revenue, average order value

  Multi-Channel Funnels. Track the full journey of customers who convert

  Attribution. Help you understand interaction between first clicks and final actions

You really must use this software. Google Analytics has so many features, it will astound you. I recently went to a seminar on Analytics and the "experts" confessed that none of them knew anyone who had used all of Analytics' features. Don't be overwhelmed. Focus on what means the most to you such as incoming traffic data, exit pages, bounce rates, ad performance, value per visit, user flow, page speed, social media referrals, conversion rates, and so on.

Wrap Up

Google Analytics is amazing. Use it. The free version has more than enough features for most businesses.

Chapter 37: Customer Relationship Management (CRM)

CRM software is typically hosted in the cloud and is used for managing an organization's relationships and interactions with customers and potential customers. With CRM, salespeople, their sales managers, and marketers track sales opportunities as they move through the pipeline.

Before today's widespread adoption of the cloud, customer relationships were largely maintained by sales representatives on their personal laptops, using Outlook and Lotus Notes platforms, some of which still are used today. Today, it's almost mandatory to use a CRM. Salesforece.com is the market leader.

Since the dawn of time, sales forecasting has been a grey and murky arena. See Sales Forcasting Chapter for a simple, highly effective sales forecasting method. The certainty to which a customer is willing to pay large sums for a purchase has always been difficult to predict and as the purchase sums go higher, the number of required signatures and qualifications and discounts applied also increase, creating a wholly complex process to scoring a sale. Today, despite the existence of many tools and technologies, sales forecasting remains tricky. Even though sales representatives are still likely to keep some big deals close to the cuff, and critical customer information to themselves, while obfuscating their sales numbers to keep sales management at arm length, transparency in the overall process has improved from the old days.

Data Matters

At the heart of the problem lies data—customer contact data, customer account data, and data on the different transactions a sales representative may have with a customer or potential customer. Maintaining this data and using it in strategic and meaningful ways is what customer relationship management is all about. Customer contact data, account data and transactional data and even general knowledge on a customer becomes part of the customer record and is augmented every time a new interaction occurs. Data is even gathered on customers who aren't yet customers but are likely to become one.

Prospect/customer data is used to categorize where in the sales cycle an interaction stands—the beginning, middle or the end, and where status ranks in terms of probability. Over time, sales reps are evaluated on their ability to be predictable as much as for their ability to sell and this is the genesis of how CRM systems were built and even how they operate today.

Data accuracy takes work

It might seem obvious that CRM systems are intended to keep customer contact and account data clean, but most all sales reps and sales organizations in firms large and small will tell you how difficult it is to do over time. Even monolith platforms like Salesforce, Microsoft, SAP, and Oracle are plagued with data that gets dirty over time, must be cleaned periodically, and maintained even with the help of third-party validating services like Dunn & Bradstreet. This is because contacts (customers, employees, and clients) tend to move around, jump from one customer to another or will switch roles within a firm changing the nature of a relationship.

Adding to the data problem is the fact that companies (entities) can be represented so many ways in a system. Think of AT&T as a prime example. Very few people might refer to it by its official name Atlantic Telephone and Telegraph Inc. Most would call it AT&T, but if your system doesn't handle special characters well, then some might abbreviate it as ATT or ATandT. Or even AT. Deciding *how* information is to be stored in a database is as important as *what* information goes into it.

More than data stores

There are different ways to capture the nature of a relationship, the behaviors that influence it, and the external and internal forces unique to a firm that enable or endanger the possibility of a sale. In the 20 years that CRM has become its own certified science, the data collected has become its greatest asset and spawned newer areas of discovery such as business intelligence and KPIs (key performance indicators) and predictive analytics based on sophisticated data analysis. The data lives beyond static reports and simple number crunching.

Data has evolved into living and dynamic dashboards that are capable of slicing and dicing and drilling into data in any shape or form and according to the unique needs of a business. These days, companies big and small rely on real time analysis of the data within their own systems to create uniquely tailored sales processes to target clients.

Relationship management

CRM has evolved into relationship management programs that have graduated well beyond customers and the sales process. The same benefits that have been realized by CRM systems have now been applied to new kinds of systems adapted to industries and business models that aren't sales based. Volunteer Relationship Management, Partner Relationship and Supplier Relationship Management are new offshoot examples of how the same principles of capturing contacts entities and interactions and then analyzing data in real time can help for-profit and non-profit entities run themselves more efficiently.

Wrap Up

Without CRM you're doing battle with bows and arrows while others have a high-powered rifle.

Chapter 38: Big Data

Data-dominated firms are going to take market share, customers, and profits away from those who are still relying too heavily on their human experts.

- Andrew McAfee
MIT Digital Research Scientist

Very few small companies are enjoying the benefits of big data and the opportunity to mine data on customer behaviors and market trends. That's because such data analysis requires expensive hardware and software, consultants, and huge amounts of time to invest in analytics. But trends such as cloud computing, open-source software, and software-as-a-service (SAAS) are changing all that. New, inexpensive ways to learn from data are emerging all the time.

Rent instead of buy is one answer. For example, at kaggle.com, you can put data scientists to work for you. Data brokers such as Acxiom and Data Logix can provide companies with extremely valuable data at reasonable prices. Open database firm Factual is building datasets around health care, education, entertainment, and government. Renting is a lot cheaper than buying.

Google Trends is another way to utilize Big Data. Google Trends showcases trending topics by quantifying how often a search term is entered relative to the total search volume. Marketers can stay informed on what topics are cool, hip, popular, and relevant.

Global marketers can assess the popularity of certain topics across countries or languages.

Bigger Data

One of the biggest challenges to face organizations of the modern era is what to do with all the data they are gathering. It seems all firms these days aspire to be "technology" firms and since nearly all interactions (transactions) are now online, even for brick and mortar stores, the interaction data has become an asset within itself. Because data is a perpetually growing vast ocean, it commonly denoted as "Big Data" or even as a "data lake."

Data is generated whenever an activity or interaction occurs. In the old days, this data was captured manually by bookkeepers and shop owners and by CPAs. Invoices and receipts were handwritten. Then came the tech revolution and business data and purchase data began to be stored into spreadsheets and databases which were stored on local servers or in large data centers. And then the cloud happened, and data began to be stored centrally, aggregated across firms, analyzed, and dissected to find patterns and correlations.

Old Science

Scientists have used data analysis techniques forever. In order to understand physics and biology and chemistry, even sociology, where data is especially important for inferring insights about humans, statistics have been used to prove or disprove theories. It is the quality of inference, which is central to the value of Big Data. On its own, gathering data has little value, however, when data can be used to gain insights, and to predict human behavior, it then gains special value.

Interaction data as well as demographic data can indeed be of great value to a company. The more companies understand the habits and behaviors of their audience and users, the more companies can provide customized products and services. This would seem to be a benefit to all; however, this type of data also skirts a fine line between ascertaining insights with altruistic intentions versus an invasion of privacy.

Privacy

Not all users want to be targeted for certain products because it might compromise their identity or personal information. Let's consider a problem that affects a large amount of the population. As they age, people tend to face health problems such as diabetes, high blood pressure or erectile dysfunction or infertility. Most might be willing to discuss these matters privately with a doctor, but if they happen to purchase products online, and this information is collected, saved, and attributed to a customer, then that knowledge can be used against them. That customer may now face possible embarrassment, discrimination, harassment or simply be annoyed by psychological reminders of their malady by different kinds of marketing or content targeting. This is often why customer rights are brought up and often customers disable targeting by websites or social media platforms to stay anonymous versus facing an invasion as platforms and systems increasingly share data about their customers with third parties.

In the 80s and 90s, many firms discriminated against its LGBTQ workforce and forced employees to hide and remain in the closet. Many might remember the groundbreaking film *Philadelphia*, which broke through social norms of the time. It was not until well into the new millennia that LGBTQ communities gained back some basic human rights only with the help of the Supreme Court and a tide of change in culture. One of the key figures to help normalize and create new social norms was Ellen Degeneres. Even today, those in the community are not anxious to be exposed for fear of retaliation or consequences because of their choices. This same scenario stands to play out for people who do not wish to expose certain other facets about themselves to companies. This is especially true of medical conditions that might risk protections or have insurance coverage ramifications.

Making it meaningful

With the aggregation of large volumes of transactional and demographic data comes inherent problems such as faulty or incomplete data. These holes or gaps in data can result in an unclear picture about any desired segment. This is often referred to as "noisy" data or "unclean" data because drawing clear conclusions is difficult or finding exact results to any query becomes a difficult exercise. Therefore, many products and services are offered in today's landscape to "clean" data, fill in the gaps or reduce "noise" from irrelevant data. This is a growing science that goes back to traditional techniques used in statistics to determine if relevancy exists or a correlation can be made between data points. Statistically relevant data requires the data to be clean and to be factually correct and often it is difficult to know if data is in fact factually correct. Demographic data like sex and age, makes it simpler, although not guaranteed, but when considering secondary demographic data such as marriage or address or employment, this picture gets murkier. People lie.

Cyber Security

Personal information can also be misused to open credit cards, make large purchases or loans, and devastate or ruin someone financially. For these reasons, the government in the recent decade has sought to penalize companies who abuse personal data. PII or Personally Identifiable Information must be managed very carefully by firms and audited periodically to be compliant to government laws. This is especially true of the federal government. Maintaining data integrity and keeping it away from those who seek to abuse it is what has launched the field of Cyber Security. Common terminology in this burgeoning field include intrusion detection, antivirus, malware, vulnerability scanning and exploitation (passive), threat detection and threat hunting (active), cyber hygiene, firewalls, anomalies, alerts, and risk mitigation. Cyber warfare is a new field of attack because it can paralyze firms, agencies and even countries without physical expenditure of lives and combat.

Business Intelligence

As if privacy invasion wasn't enough of a concern, then there is the widespread use of targeted advertising that seems to exist everywhere as soon as a purchase is made. This simple act of making an online purchase triggers hundreds of advertisers to descend upon you, advertise to you, inundate you, whether you asked for it or not. Anonymity seems to be fast disappearing.

Corporations use data to guide their decision-making process around product development and service offerings and this is fueled by advertisements, market analysis, and comparison of competitive landscapes. Called "Business Intelligence", corporations use it for navigating their business terrain, to recruit and determine the type of skills and technologies that deserve further investigation, so that they can capitalize on the next big trend and draw in new customers or to pull the maximum benefit/value from its own existing customer base. Business Intelligence aims to allow businesses to run lean and shrewdly, with maximum efficiency and without wasting resources and budget. Business Intelligence also allows corporations to gain historical perspective which can be a useful guide for future trends and response strategies.

Based on historical trends, consumer patterns, market fluctuations, demand and supply and technology evolution, a business can be smart about when and how and where to make its investments, how long to keep chasing a goal, or decide to abandon a strategy if it doesn't yield desired performance metrics. That's why business metrics and business intelligence are closely tied and always evolving. A business in today's world is a continually adapting and learning entity and its leadership is rewarded or punished for how well it acts and performs against its data analysis and future predictions.

Predictive Analytics

One of the most important areas of research in big data and business intelligence is predictive analytics. Put simply, it is the science predicting human behaviors or outcomes based on past behaviors or patterns. In school, we all learned about causal events—those outcomes that can be traced back to an event or a predicating circumstance. Causal relationships are hard to find in data unless there is direct correlation. Very often, human behavior is not causal, or there are enough intervening data points to make determining the initial trigger event (or circumstance) leading to an outcome, very difficult. However, the greater the likelihood or an action/reaction causal relationship, the greater the "confidence level" in the relevance of the data and its correlation. This is the premise and the promise of predictive analytics. By analyzing thousands if not millions, even billions of interactions and events, possible correlations gain higher levels of confidence leading to the ability to confidently predict that an event or interaction will lead to another. This is especially helpful to predict if a customer will buy that product or service, sign up for a subscription, be willing to pay a certain amount, stay loyal to a brand, abandon a sale, try a new product, or simply walk away.

Wrap Up

Create corporate procedures and procure enough technology tools to ensure that business, product, customer, and market data are captured, analyzed, and well managed.

Chapter 39: Amazon and Alibaba

In the old world, you devoted 30% of your time to building a great product/service and 70% of your time to shouting about it. In the new world, that inverts

- Jeff Bezos
Amazon Founder and CEO

Help young people. Help small guys. Because small guys will be big. Young people will have the seeds you bury in their minds, and when they grow up, they will change the world.

- Jack Ma
Alibaba Founder

AMAZON (*Amazon.com*) is the world's largest online retailer and a prominent cloud services provider. Based in Seattle, Washington, the company hosts and manages the world's largest e-commerce marketplace.

Just about anyone or any company can sell products (theirs or anyone's) on Amazon. In many cases, sellers (called Retail Arbitrators) buy products from somewhere at a very low price, mark them up, and advertise them on Amazon. They then take the orders directly from the buyers and handle the entire transaction (handling the money, shipping the products, and providing customer services). In this case, Amazon acts as a middleman, but does monitor how well the seller performs (on time delivery, reviews, and so on). Amazon charges these sellers transaction and monthly fees.

For trademarked brand owners, Amazon can take a more proactive role with a program called Fulfillment by Amazon (FBA). Here, Amazon stores the trademarked owner's products at Amazon Fulfillment centers all over the world. When a customer decides to buy an FBA product, Amazon finds the product in their warehouse, packages it, ships it to the customer, collects the money and sends the seller a commission check every two weeks or so.

Buy Box

The Buy Box is the little blue box to the right of each product detail screen on Amazon. It houses Amazon's most important real estate, the Add to Cart button. Almost all Amazon shoppers, when they decide to buy the featured product, click on this button.

Amazon decides which seller is tied to the button at any one time. That seller will get 90 percent of the orders for that product. Other vendors are listed below the button.

Therefore, your number one sales goal is to get Amazon to choose you as the featured vendor in the Buy Box. To increase your chances of getting chosen, you'll need to be priced competitively (being lowest price really helps), have great customer service, offer Prime and free shipping, and always have stock on hand ready to ship. Do some research and take the time to figure it all out. It's worth your time.

Too Big to Ignore

Even if you're an arbitrager, buying low and selling high, or you own the brand and have a registered trademark, Amazon is worth trying. It's reach, reputation and marketing power are unmatched and something you really need to put into your sales and marketing toolkit.

Amazon also offers a two-day, delivery service called Amazon Prime that has over 100 million subscribers worldwide. And it has a publishing arm (*The Washington Post*), a film and television studio, and owns Whole Foods. It also provides one of the world's largest cloud computing platforms through its Amazon Web Services (AWS) subsidiary.

ALIBABA (*alibaba.com*) is a marketplace that connects Business-to-Business (B2B) sellers and buyers all over the world. Jack Ma started the company in 1999. With headquarters in Hangzhou, China, Alibaba has become the tenth largest company in the world. With ten million active buyers (which they define as customers who have made purchase in the last 30 days), Alibaba has over 150,000 sellers, mostly based in China and Asia.

B2B all over the World

As of 2020, the company has a program to enable US manufacturers to become Alibaba.com sellers. For an annual fee, they build the manufacturer a mini store site that will run on Alibaba and provide buyers with everything they need to make a purchase. The actual transaction takes place between buyer and seller. Alibaba is the middleman and does not take a commission on sales.

Think of Alibaba as an online trade show. Your booth (Alibaba calls it your mini site) is there for prospects to view. If they stop there (click) they get a better look at what you sell and can leave you a message. Here is where some magic occurs. For one, if your visitor is from a country that doesn't speak your native language, Alibaba will automatically change the text on your mini site to one your visitor speaks. And, if the visitor leaves a message in his native tongue, Alibaba will translate it into your language. Likewise, they translate your messages back to the visitor. Further, Alibaba ranks your visitors. If your visitor regularly makes lots of inquires with numerous sellers, but doesn't buy, his rating is low. If, however, your visitor is only looking at what you sell and has a record of doing business, you should pay attention.

Alibaba uses its Global Gold Supplier Rating to rank its suppliers. Each supplier gets a ranking based on three major aspects: products, service, and marketing capability.

Product capability is measure by two indicators: number of products available to buyers and product information (how well the products are described on Alibaba).

Service capability is measured by one indicator: how quickly the seller responds to a request from a buyer inquiry.

Marketing capability is measure by two indicators: number of active visitors and the number of visitors who click on the seller's ads.

Each indicator has 5 levels (5 stars the highest, 1 star the lowest). The lowest star rating of all five determines the overall star rating of the supplier. There are predetermined thresholds for each star rankings, for example, 30 active visitors earns 3 stars; 50 earns 4 stars.

Alibaba uses its star rankings to determine each supplier's search ranking and overall visibility to prospective buyers

In all, Alibaba provides small US businesses with product sources as well as an outlet to sell products to B2B customers at home and abroad. Here is a way to market and sell all over the globe, without ever getting on an airplane. In 2019, the world-wide B2B market was estimated at $23.9 trillion. For information about becoming an Alibaba seller, go to www.alibaba.com and click on Join Free and follow directions. You can join as a Buyer or Seller or both

Wrap Up

Buy something on Amazon. Get a sense of how it works and what works best. Most of the top sellers really know how to do it right. Then, try selling something on Amazon. If that works, investigate FBA.

Join Alibaba as a buyer at least. There are some extraordinary bargains on there, from sellers all over the world.

Chapter 40: Beyond Your Website

How many eyes you attract to your website is certainly one measure of success on the Internet. Especially when those eyes belong to people who are sincerely interested in what you have to offer.

People are interested in people. Social networks have gained extraordinary popularity. These attractive, interactive mediums invite customer involvement. Get involved. Respond to questions personally. Solicit feedback. Inviting customer involvement and embracing business transparency can only help your business grow and stay ahead of the competition.

Content travels virally from site to site. Before long, your Facebook page, LinkedIn profile, blog and Tweets will start to find their own audience without expensive ads or other traditional forms of business promotion. Keep content fresh because it generates "stickiness" from customers.

YouTube is another opportunity to propagate your message. YouTube lets anyone embed, or paste, a video into their own blog or website. User-generated content—especially video—gets the largest audiences. However, there are no controls on what gets posted and where it's posted. Make sure what you say does you justice, isn't offensive, and doesn't reveal any inside information.

Your current and future customers are probably already plugged in and interested in what you have to say.

Technology marches on. Meanwhile new terminology and technologies abound.

Terminology	Translation	What it means
Viral, Viral Marketing	The name for the phenomenon that occurs when an idea or Internet asset, like a video, gets propagated from person to person via word-of-mouth personal suggestion.	Bad news becomes viral quickly; but so does an enticing idea, story, or video. Email already does this to an extent—as when people forward jokes and such to friends. Viral marketing exploits web behavior specifically.
User generated content	Content generated by users on blogs or sometimes videos made with camcorders or phones	Advertisers get nervous about using sites with user-generated content for liability reasons, but popularity is causing advertisers to pay attention. It's like reality TV for advertisers.

Content Management	Refers to the warehousing and cataloging of content for the purposes of consumption by a system or website	When websites get large or they specialize in the art of generating content, they require the content to be cataloged so that it can be searched and found easily.

Wrap Up

In the end, sales and marketing is a people business. Use today's and tomorrow's technologies to do what sales and marketing is all about. Identify new prospects, qualify them, close them, and turn them into perpetual customers.

WRAP UP

Chapter 41: Contingencies

I have accomplished almost nothing on the first,
second or even third try.
It's called chutzpah, and it works.

- Jerry Weintraub
American Film Producer

What could go wrong?

Risks come with the territory. Sometimes you even create your own risk by being too aggressive. At some point in time, most companies are faced with a difficult issue such as running short of cash, discovering the market is too small, or having a product that doesn't sell well.

Running out of Money

What will you do if you run out of cash? What can you do now to ensure additional cash would be available? Is it possible to accelerate those portions of your business that offer the potential for the earliest positive cash flow?

Here is a very good practice to follow. Assume you only have one-half the amount of money you really have and rewrite your expense budget accordingly.

Which expenses could you reduce now before you encounter a cash flow problem?
What aspects of your business could be accelerated to expedite the arrival of cash?
What aspects of your business could be curtailed to reduce cash outlays?
Where and how could you raise additional cash?
Other ideas?

Not Enough Customers

What would cause demand for your product to wane? Recession? New technology? New competition? Is there some way to lock-in your existing customers? Are there new territories, resellers, or even new markets for your product?

What will you do if the market goes soft?
What can you do to keep up with the market's changing needs?
Try being much more precise in your targeting, that is, narrow your focus by emphasizing one aspect of your offer. You specialize in these kinds of situations. For these customers, you're the market leader.

Mediocre Product

What can you change about the product? Can you add features or services? What about bundling or lowering the price? Can you reduce your costs to make/deliver the product or service?

What will you do if your product doesn't sell as well as planned?
Try what we used to call "mid-life kickers". That is, improve the offer by adding something extra, maybe some free services, or more lenient purchase terms, or free trial, and so on.

Other

What else could possibly go wrong?

Wrap Up

You can learn a few things about your business and have fun by doing unrestrained brainstorming on what could go wrong. Ask anyone whose opinion matters to you what those things might be. As crazy as some of them might sound at first, they could point to potential challenges.

Chapter 42: Fast-Pass Worksheet

You need to define your target market and your target audience. You need to be clear as to what makes your products different and what problems your products solve for them. You need to specify how they can find out about you and your products and how they can conveniently buy what you sell.

However, before you really get into all this, first make sure your business model works, that is, put together a P&L proforma, which is described early in this book. So first,

What's the business model? How does it make money? Need a proforma income statement.

Who's it for? Create at least two or three personas. What does your product do? What problems are you solving in the life of the customer? What will make the customer feel good about buying your product? What's in it for the customer? Can you monetize his/her benefit?

What's the market? Smaller the better. Think of a bell curve. Your place is at the far left: where do needs are not yet being satisfied.

What makes you different? This is what a competitor's star salesperson asked me as I was trying to convince him to join our company. It's all he wanted to know. He knew that if what made us different wasn't important to the people he would be calling on; we weren't the right company for him or his customers.

How will customers purchase your product? From your salespeople, distributors, retailers, over the Internet, over the phone?

Why should the customer believe you? What references can you provide? Do you have a persuasive demonstration?

Who is the competition? Why would prospects buy from them and not you? Why you not them? See question 1 above.

How/where can I find the best prospects? If it's advertising, where will you run the ad? If it's the Internet, what will they be asking the search engines? If it's target accounts, forget about advertising, go set up camp right in their lobby.

Digital marketing. Website, social media plan.

How will you turn your new customers into perpetual customers and reference accounts? Will your follow-up personally or by phone? Who is responsible? Can you provide prompt, knowledgeable post-sales support? How can you ensure that all your customer info is stored, current, and accessible?

Author Bios

William D. Hughes has more than forty years of professional sales, marketing, and business management experience. He has held executive level positions with large and small companies. Since 1990 he has worked with 50 plus small-to-medium-size companies to increase revenues, profits, and corporate valuation through time-efficient, innovative business strategies, coupled with results-driven sales and marketing programs.

Bill has authored two books on Sales & Marketing, *How to Avoid Critical Mistakes* and *Sales & Marketing Action Plan.* He attended Ocean College in New Jersey and the University of Virginia. He has been a guest lecturer at Rutgers University in New Brunswick, New Jersey and National University in San Diego, California. Bill joined the USMC right after high-school and rose to the position of Sergeant.

Michael Hughes has been in the digital marketing field since 1999. He has helped thousands of businesses increase sales and realize profitable returns from their online marketing investments.

Finding prospective buyers for businesses of all sizes and shapes has given him insider access to some of our nation's most innovative and successful entrepreneurs. That experience along with his technical prowess have made him a highly sought-after online business consultant.

Michael specializes in Search Engine Optimization and Marketing, Paid Search Advertising, and Conversion Optimization. He received a bachelor's degree in Marketing from Sonoma State University.

Aastha Verma is a graduate of the University of Maryland at College Park, where she received her bachelor's degree in electrical engineering and a master's in system engineering.

Her company, Project Rescue Consulting.com specializes in translating concepts into deliverables to help companies, particularly start-ups, transform their visions into market-ready products.

Aastha has also consulted for the federal government on cross collaborative and cloud-based platforms for cybersecurity applications. And she has been helping them adopt emerging cloud technologies as they transform and modernize legacy systems and architecture.

She is also a regular commentator on a nationally syndicated Indian news and opinion program. She is well connected with the movers and shakers in the Indian community who provide IT services or are liaisons to Fortune 100 companies across the country.

www.ingramcontent.com/pod-product-compliance
Lightning Source LLC
Chambersburg PA
CBHW021923190326
41519CB00009B/886